Civic Center

Praise for **Viral Explosions!**

"Viral Explosions is brilliantly simple and simply brilliant! Peggy McColl, whose marketing genius I've admired for years, gives away all of her online marketing secrets in this book. I encourage you to read it and apply the wisdom contained within these pages—you'll be happy you did!"

—Marci Shimoff, *New York Times* best-selling author of *Happy for No Reason* and *Chicken Soup for the Woman's Soul*, and featured teacher in *The Secret*

"If you want to live life on your own terms, this is your guidebook to help you get there!"

—Rick Frishman, founder of Planned TV Arts, Publisher Morgan James Publishing

"Peggy McColl has done it again! Viral Explosions is the Rosetta Stone for anyone who wants to conceptualize, plan, and implement a viral marketing campaign. Take it from someone who has done it – over and over again. If you're serious about success, your copy of Viral Explosions will quickly become as highlighted and dog-eared as mine is."

—Joe Tye, author of *The Florence Prescription* and *All Hands on Deck*

"Viral Explosions! brings readers the full depth of Peggy's vast experience as an innovator in Internet marketing, and Peggy thoughtfully reiterates as always that passion, a powerful message, and core value are basic and quintessential to any plan's design destined for success."

—Bryan C. Flournoy, *Making It All Click* Visionary Series

"As someone who works on marketing daily, I can honestly say this is the best resource guide I have found yet. It is laced with Peggy's wisdom that has been gained through the experience of successful marketing over the past 10 years for some of today's most successful visionaries. Its simple, easy-to-follow format allows the reader to visualize an instant game plan. This book is it for any human being who desires to successfully market anything online or offline."

—Lauren E. Miller, best-selling author of
Hearing His Whisper

"Knowledge is cheap these days. All of us can set up a blog, shoot a movie, publish a book, twitter like a fiend. But getting people to see your stuff? That's tricky. Everyone's overwhelmed by the content everyone else is creating. To be seen you need a plan. And Peggy McColl's Viral Explosions! gives you that plan. You still need to create something amazing and you will need to work hard to to put this plan into effect. But do all that and follow Peggy's plan, and you're going to be seen and heard and read. You're going to be known."

—Michael Bungay Stanier, author of *Do More Great Work*
and creator of *The Eight Irresistible Principles of Fun*

Viral Explosions!

Proven Techniques to Expand, Explode, or Ignite Your Business or Brand Online

By Peggy McColl

CAREER PRESS

Franklin Lakes, NJ

VIRAL EXPLOSIONS!
Edited by Kate Henches
Typeset by Diana Ghazzawi
Cover design by Howard Grossman/12E Design
Printed in the U.S.A. by Courier

To order this title, please call toll-free 1-800-CAREER-1 (NJ and
Can-ada: 201-848-0310) to order using VISA or MasterCard, or for
further information on books from Career Press.

The Career Press, Inc., 3 Tice Road, PO Box 687,
Franklin Lakes, NJ 07417
www.careerpress.com
Library of Congress Cataloging-in-Publication Data
McColl, Peggy, 1958-
Viral explosions : proven techniques to expand, explode, or ignite
    your business or brand online / by Peggy McColl.
        p. cm.
    Includes index.
ISBN 978-1-60163-119-0 – ISBN 978-1-60163-746-8 (ebook)
    1. Internet marketing. 2. Branding (Marketing) --
Management. I. Title.
HF5415.1265.M344 2010
381'.142--dc22
                                                    2010003378

31232009071293

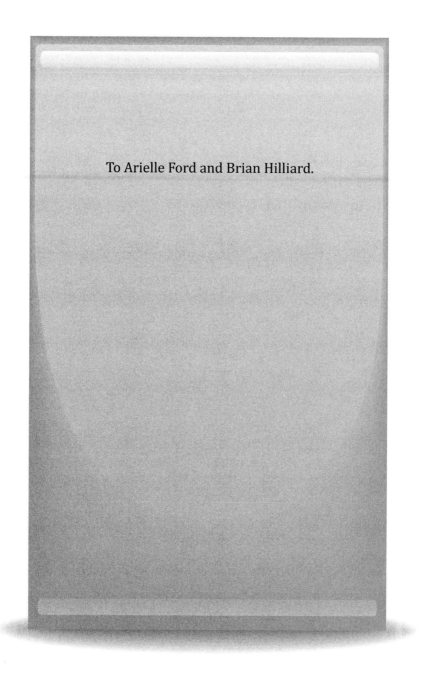

To Arielle Ford and Brian Hilliard.

Acknowledgments

As I sat down to write this section for the book, knowing the importance of the information in *Viral Explosions*, I was challenged to keep the acknowledgment section to a length that is reasonable...which is a very good thing.

I have so many people to thank...starting with you the reader. If it weren't for you, there would be no book. If it weren't for you, there would be no viral explosions of any kind. Think about it: We all need people to help us, and to that end we can make a positive difference in the lives of millions of others.

Let me start by acknowledging my wonderful and talented ghostwriter, Nancy Peske. Nancy and I have been through so much together. We have created several books together, and during that time we have both lost our parents. In each situation, our parents were ill and required care for a period of time prior to their departing, and when you have deadlines to meet, and emotional challenges, and you are stretched by commitments, it can be challenging. Nancy and I always met our commitments and stayed true to our priorities (our family) while we were taking care of business. Nancy is a blessing in my life, and I'm deeply grateful for her. She's wonderfully talented (you probably already know that if you have read any of my other books, and she is also a deeply caring woman, who cares about you, the reader, and she cares that the messages are delivered in the most effective way). Nancy, from my heart to yours, thank you!

Of course, the book wouldn't even be in the hands of a publisher if it wasn't for my loving and devoted agent, Cathy Hemming. She's another gift in my life, and not only is she my cherished agent, she's also a valued friend.

My sister, Judy O'Beirn, has been a huge support with this book (and all of my books, for that matter). For that, I'm grateful. Judy also heads up a team of extraordinary people who are all part of Hasmark Services, Inc. They live by their motto— the Heart and Soul of Marketing—and have helped me tremendously to create "best-seller" status for many of my books. Judy is supported by the lovely Jenn Gibson, Amy Lusk, Sandy Batten, and Yvonne Higham, and I'm grateful for their endless support and giving nature.

Career Press, the publisher for this book, showed instant enthusiasm for *Viral Explosions*. They believe in the book and the message and have invested in making this book a priority for their promotional activities. It is a wonderful, warm feeling knowing your publisher is fully behind the author's message. I appreciate their dedication and commitment and have overwhelming gratitude toward them.

This book is dedicated to my good friends Arielle Ford and Brian Hilliard. One evening while having dinner in San Diego with Arielle and Brian, I mentioned the concept for my book and explained it was like an "online ripple" (which is the name I originally intended for the book), and Brian said "Isn't that like a viral explosion?" Well, the rest is history, as they say. Thank you both for your inspiration, your friendship, and your support.

As always, both my son, Michel, and my husband, Denis, offer continual support and are beside me all the way. My life is abundantly rich because they are in it!

With all my love and heart felt appreciation,

Peggy

Contents

Foreword

There aren't many surprises left in the world of books—not to me, that is. I read about 15 books a month, write a bunch myself, blog, flog, and do whatever else I can do to let off my creative steam in whatever way seems important to me at the time.

All of which leads me up to the reason I am writing this Foreword for Peggy McColl's latest book.

It is remarkable.

Remarkably written, remarkably researched, remarkably entertaining, remarkably surprising, and remarkably comprehensive for anyone who is determined to do what Peggy herself has done: achieved tremendous success in book selling, product promotion, brand development, and Internet marketing.

You truly need to take this book in.

Of course, it's not just about tricks you can do.

More often, it's about imagination beyond the call of duty. It's about how to paint a paperclip red and call it a new color of blue.

It's about how to name a whale, or even a giant, without being embarrassed by what you do.

It's about reaching around corners to discover your other hand, and when you've done that, shaking it, and saying hello without doubting yourself. It's about being bold and creative.

In Peggy's book, you've just got to let them flow.

The ideas, that is.

It's not just about selling; it's about exploding into a new space, a place you've never been before, and Peggy is right next to you, encouraging you and asking you the question: Are you enjoying yourself yet?

How does one woman come up with so many remarkably exciting and stimulating ways to fly, climb, run, and paddle all the way to success?

What possesses such a woman as Peggy McColl?

Where, I continually asked myself as I read and explored the delightful pages of this book, does this lady get her juice?

What improbable store did she buy it in?

I've got to go there myself, I think.

And you too have got to go there, dear reader.

Because your life will never be the same again.

Thank you, Peggy McColl, for an absolutely joyful book!

—Michael E. Gerber

author of *The E-Myth* books and
The Most Successful Small Business in the World

The Origin of My Recipe for *Viral Explosions!*

Viral marketing: Marketing on the Internet that spreads a message rapidly

Viral explosion: An extremely rapid spread of information via the Internet that yields extraordinary results

The books were everywhere: on the floor, piled up in huge stacks, underneath the dining room table, snaking out into the hallway. In my eagerness to express my ideas to the world, I had written my very first book, *On Being the Creator of Your Destiny*, had it self-published, printed, and bound, and ordered 3,000 copies to be delivered to my front door. Now the UPS truck was driving away and it was dawning on me that I'd better start selling these babies! But how? I didn't know anyone in the book business and hadn't realized that they don't just automatically place self-published books on their shelves (in fact, it's quite an uphill effort to get them there). I could have stuck a "Books for Sale!" sign on my front lawn and waited for the doorbell to ring, I suppose, but I knew my dining room would be filled with piles of books for quite some time if I took that approach. The invoices for printing, editing, and shipping were already sitting on my desk. I'd spent several months working on the book and, because I was self-employed, I hadn't been bringing in any income during that time. What's more, I was a single mom paying all my own personal and business expenses including private-school tuition for my son. So although I wasn't sure exactly how I was going to do this, I knew I had to turn those books into cash—fast!

I drew upon what I knew about Internet marketing and figured out how I might launch a viral explosion. I asked people I knew to help me out and promote my book to people on their e-mail lists. I hoped that if word got out to enough potential customers, maybe I'd break even. I found that everyone was eager to do what they could, so I crossed my fingers and hoped a few orders would come in during the 48 hours of my limited offer.

The first day, each time I heard the tone that indicated I had e-mail, I'd run over to my laptop to check it out, and sure enough, it was an order. Soon, I was hearing "bing, bing, bing," coming from the tiny speaker in my computer and I started to get excited. In fact, I placed my laptop on my nightstand so that as I slept, I could hear the reassuring "bings" that told me I had yet another e-mail, a likely order. I didn't mind waking up several times because I knew that every single "bing" meant money coming in!

The next day, the e-mails continued to pour in. I asked a neighbor to come over and we started hauling stacks of books to the living room, where we would pack up the orders going out to Canada, and to the kitchen, where we'd pack the international orders. I designated the dining room for books that would be shipped to America. My friend and I made trip after trip to the post office.

In a very short time, as a result of my Internet marketing campaign that had turned into a viral explosion, I had orders from 26 different countries, close to $30,000 in sales, radio and televisions stations calling to interview me, and offers for foreign rights. It was astonishing! Very quickly, I realized I'd hit upon a successful formula, and started launching more Internet marketing campaigns. I promoted several books and products of my own. Then I started helping other authors, from Gregg Braden to Wayne Dyer to Marianne Williamson, to launch their own Internet marketing campaigns and drive their books up the best-seller lists, including the very prestigious *New York Times* list. Publishers were calling me to ask me to help them make their books into best-sellers. I sold my book *Your Destiny Switch* to a publisher and used my viral explosion formula to make it a *New York Times* best-seller, too!

Soon, I began teaching a sold-out teleseminar course on how to make your book a best-seller, and started mentoring clients who wanted to make big money on the Internet. Having learned so much from my experiences, I'm eager to teach you how to create your very own!

By working with the program outlined in this book, you can use the Web to create information-based products and services and market them effectively so that they reach an extraordinary number of people and build your brand and your business. In fact, I believe you can use the recipe here for selling just about anything on the Internet. I truly believe that you can create a viral explosion, because if I can do it, you can. I have no specialized technical ability, no marketing degree or MBA—in fact, I never even went to college. What I do have is the three Ps you'll read about in this book—**P**assion, **P**rosperity consciousness, and **P**artners—which you, too, can attain, embrace, and use for your own benefit.

You may be an established entrepreneur who simply wants to make extra income and boost your revenue and customer base. You might have a cause you're eager to promote, or products and services you believe can help others solve a problem, and you want to know how to do a time- and cost-effective outreach. You may be determined to make large amounts of money so that you don't have to work quite so hard and can spend more time with your family, friends, and pets, or do more traveling or charitable work. Here's a reassuring truth: *You do not have to know what it is you want to sell in order to create a viral explosion on the Internet.*

In this book, you'll learn to tap into your creativity, passion, and optimism so that ideas come to you easily and you'll soon figure out what it is you want to promote and who your potential customers might be. You'll start to envision where you want to go and the path will begin to reveal itself. Ideas for more products, more promotions, and more viral explosions will come to you. You'll even find a glossary of the italicized terms at the back of the book.

So let's get started exploring all the elements of creating a hugely successful viral explosion!

Chapter 1

You Can Launch a Viral Explosion!

Are you living from your passion, or are you settling for the life you think you have to lead?

I believe we all have a passion, even if we haven't discovered it yet. When our work is aligned with our passion, then we're operating with rocket fuel.

Whatever your passion, you can tap into it to create a product, service, or offering that will benefit others, then launch it into the stratosphere using the Internet. You can create a viral explosion.

Most people have something to promote, even if it's just a funny video they made that they believe will inspire or amuse others. If you've got a product to sell or a service to offer, you've probably wished your message could rush through the Internet with all the speed and excitement of the Susan Boyle "Britain's Got Talent" audition video. We all know the potential to "go viral" and reach millions of people is enormous, but how can you do it? The secret is to create a great product, to make your promotional copy irresistible, to partner with people who can help you reach a mass audience instantly, and to have a plan.

An emotionally engaging video of a singer, or a lion hugging his former human owners, or a man who discovered that fast-food hamburgers take months to spoil, gets passed along like wildfire because:

1. It has strong emotional appeal.

2. It seems fresh and new, like something you've never seen before.

3. It asks you to take immediate action (to watch it, to visit a certain Website, and so on).

4. People want to share something of value and interest with other people they know.

These four types of appeal are behind successful Internet marketing for everything from teleseminars to eCourses, books and eBooks, jewelry, astrology readings, Webinars, t-shirts, mentoring services, software applications, and a million other products and services that have a potentially huge audience. Your viral explosion will generate excitement because it's being recommended person to person, via e-mails, social media, existing social networks, and other online methods. It will contain an offer that speaks to people's emotions, that feels new or different in some way, and that creates a sense of urgency, encouraging recipients to act now.

Once you know the recipe for designing an irresistible offer and setting off a viral explosion, you can use that formula again and again, combining the elements in different ways so that you can build your brand and business and get your message out there. Although the Internet is always changing and new technologies, applications, software, and services crop up all the time, the techniques offered in this book are timeless. They're like the staple ingredients in your kitchen that you combine in different ways to create a recipe for success. The ideas in this book are all based on sound, proven marketing principles, which is why I'll often point out an offline example of how a particular technique has been used effectively.

I truly believe in an approach to Internet marketing that uses the power of spreading a message from person to person, because I've seen it work again and again.

Viral explosions are extremely exciting because they can have an impact far beyond what you might have imagined. They can launch you from living paycheck to paycheck to being the master of your own financial destiny. They can take you from unknown to having a highly recognizable brand. Their potential to change your life and business is amazing.

Here are three viral explosions that took off beyond anyone's expectations, all very different from each other, but all combining the elements of a successful viral explosion. They involved a red paper clip, a whale with a silly name, and an eBook of advice from self-growth experts.

Viral Explosion #1: The Red Paper Clip

Kyle MacDonald made an offer in his *blog* to trade a red paperclip to someone with an interesting item to swap, and in time, the swaps became quirkier and more valuable. People started swapping expensive items because they saw that there was increasing attention being paid to his stunt, and they wanted to get in on the story and shine the spotlight on their own causes. In one year's time, Kyle had made enough trades to be able to say he was the proud owner of a house in Saskatchewan!

Does this story make you laugh? The elements of humor and entertainment value were strong in this viral explosion. People told other people about it because they were eager to hear about the next installment. And the project was partici-patory: You could act now by making your own offer to trade something to Kyle McDonald, or you could pass it along to someone else and amuse and intrigue him or her.

Viral Explosion #2: Mr. Splashy Pants

Greenpeace, the international nonprofit organization, had a plan to put a microchip in a whale and track its movements to draw attention to the illegal whale hunting that was reduc-ing the whale population. To get people excited and involved, they started a poll to name the whale they would track. They figured people would choose a dignified name that fit the seriousness of their cause, but were surprised to see that, thanks in large part to the efforts of some bloggers, people in large numbers were insisting that the whale be dubbed "Mr. Splashy Pants." The more Greenpeace resisted the name, the faster word spread on the Internet about the possibility of naming the whale "Mr. Splashy Pants." In the end, so many people voted for this silly name that Greenpeace relented, and to their surprise, the publicity from the campaign put so much pressure on the whale hunters that they actually called off the hunt. Even better, Greenpeace was able to sell t-shirts, mugs, and bumper stickers with a cartoon of a whale and the words "Save Mr. Splashy Pants," netting them revenue that hadn't expected.

This campaign, too, had all the elements of a successful viral explosion. It was entertaining, a call to action (vote for naming the whale!), had a fresh and novel angle, and invited people to get their friends to join in on the fun. Although this explosion took off in an unexpected way, it shows you that if you're open to altering your plans a bit, you might achieve even better results than you'd anticipated.

Viral Explosion #3: 101 Great Ways to Improve Your Life

David Riklan of Selfgrowth.com put together a $27 eBook of more than 400 pages called *Self-Improvement: The Top 101 Experts Who Help Us Improve Our Lives,* which included advice from 101 self-growth experts. Knowing my reputation and success in Internet marketing, he called me up and asked if I could help him sell it. I could immediately see the potential for a viral explosion, so I created a spreadsheet of potential partners and signed up 155 of them. I set up a page attached to David's Website where anyone who bought the book could go to download several free bonus gifts, then wrote copy for an e-mail that affiliates could send to their e-mail list subscribers. Finally, I wrote the copy for the landing page he was setting up, set a date for our launch, and got ready to watch the explosion.

Between that first campaign and a second one of about the same size, which I launched a month or so later, David was able to sell just under 7,000 copies of his eBook, generating $189,000 in revenue. Given the book's tremendous success, he decided to self-publish it as a traditional, physical book, and successfully sold that one via Internet marketing as well.

The offer David made was for a limited time only, appealed to people's strong desire to receive information and advice on living a better life, felt very fresh because no one had collected so much guidance from so many recognized experts before, and was passed along person to person, using e-mail lists. Nowadays, if I were to launch this campaign, I would have him not just partner with list owners who could send out e-mails, but also use all the social media sites that weren't available to us back them.

The World Wide Web connects you to huge numbers of people, in many cases instantly. If you use the proven techniques and the staples of marketing, combined into a recipe for a viral explosion, you can connect with a mass audience that will embrace your message or product!

Creating a Viral Explosion Around an Information-Based Product

One of the ways you can benefit from the remarkable viral explosion formula is that you can use it to deliver *information-based products* for low or no cost, spurring on interest in your brand, message, and business. These products can include informational audio, video, and text products, from eBooks to traditional books, to *teleseminars* and *Webinars,* to newsletter services and "by subscription only" clubs, to mentoring, coaching, and consulting packages, all of which you'll learn how to create in this book. These products can be designed, produced, and sold or given away, in most cases, with only a very minimal financial investment. In an age of information, your expertise may have tremendous value! So, even if you are selling physical products, I hope you'll consider creating a viral explosion around an information-based product as well!

The *Viral Explosions!* Program

Viral Explosions! isn't meant to be an encyclopedia of every single tool an Internet marketer can use (although I have plenty of ideas to offer, and have an appendix with extra suggestions for promotion if you'd like to expand your strategy further). The basic elements of the formula, which can be combined in many different ways and expanded upon just like a recipe with many variations, are:

- ~   Create your brand.
- ~   Set up a Website.
- ~   Begin and build an e-mail subscriber list.
- ~   Sign up for a shopping-cart service.

~ Design and produce a product (such as an information-based eProduct).

~ Write a landing page and put it up on the Internet.

~ Sign up affiliates to help you get the word out.

~ Offer bonus gifts.

~ Pick a launch date.

~ Set yourself up to spread the word using social media and other promotional opportunities.

~ Launch!

What I'm presenting is a basic formula or recipe that has proven to work, uses effective online *and* offline marketing techniques, and can be adapted by anyone.

Before you set up your schedule for your launch, you'll need a few things that I'll help you create or acquire:

~ ***Your own brand.*** What differentiates you and your products and services from those that others are selling? If you don't yet know what you're going to offer, that's okay. Start thinking about who *you* are, what you know, what your skills are, and what value you can offer others. Although big companies create brands all the time, most people don't realize that they can come up with their own recognizable, signature brand and set themselves apart in the marketplace. You don't have to give in to negative beliefs about how much competition is out there, or how your products have to be extremely unusual and one-of-a-kind to draw in customers. I'll help you find what's special about you and how to express that in a brand and in products and services.

~ ***Products and services.*** Technology and high-speed Internet access have created an explosion of possibilities for information-based products you can create by yourself for minimal investments of time and money, including *eProducts* that can be delivered electronically, such as audio, video, and text files. To give you just one example, a few years ago, the only way to sell a book was to work with a traditional book publisher who was willing to take on your project, or produce it yourself, then stack your self-published book in your dining room or garage, and try to get it into bookstores. Now, you can write an eBook of any length, design a cover, and get your book edited and proofread (or even ghostwritten!), and sell it through shopping cart software on your own Website. In fact, you can also sell it or give it away through eBook sites, other people's newsletters, and on others' Websites. Today, if I were creating my first book, I would do it using a *print-on-demand service* that allows you to upload your electronic file for the book to a Website and have it printed out for each individual buyer, or a few copies at a time. Although the cost per copy of the finished book can be as much as three times the cost per copy of a book that had a minimum print run, the initial investment is far less.

You have many options for creating information-based eProducts to sell or give away, including Webinars, teleseminars, audio downloads, and eCourses. You can reuse your information and sell it again: for instance, you might create an eCourse that you then turn into an eBook and audio product. If you want to sell your mentoring, coaching, or consulting services, you can now reach clients all over the world via the Internet. And if you have a product to sell and ship rather than something that can be downloaded, you still have abundant possibilities for a viral explosion, as you'll see.

~ ***Partners or Affiliates.*** We all need help to reach our goals. Even if you can only think of one or two people who might help you promote your product or service, don't worry. I've learned that creating win-win partnerships with *affiliates* is far easier than you might expect (and what's especially great is that the customer wins, too!). I'll show you whom to approach, how to get others excited about helping you, and how to set up a business model that will cause people to want to participate in creating your viral explosion. I'll also explain how, when the viral explosion involves a product for sale, everyone gets paid easily and simply using software programs readily available at low cost to you.

Every day it becomes easier to launch a successful viral explosion. A wealth of software programs allow you to accept payment or host a Webinar; new software and applications crop up suddenly, become popular, allow people to make a fortune, and then transform as users' needs and desires change, offering even more ways for people to make money. Paypal, the online service for instant payment, took off because of eBay, the online auction site where individuals could sell items from their basement or garage to strangers, but I suspect someone would have come up with this idea even if eBay hadn't have existed. Plus, many people have come up with variations on the Paypal model that others may find even more useful. The number of lucrative possibilities is truly endless. It's exciting to contemplate all the new ways people will invent that will help you get your message out there. It only gets better from here!

How Easy Is It to Launch a Viral Explosion?

There's a saying that if you do what you love, the money will follow, but I don't believe it's *quite* that simple. There's a lot of hard work involved, but doors that lead to big money are plentiful. The Internet provides you access to an astonishing number of people who may be interested in what you have to sell, say, or promote, and the number of users is constantly growing. Consider that according to the Miniwatts Marketing group, 1.7 billion people worldwide have Internet access as of the writing of this book. Here's the breakdown by continent:

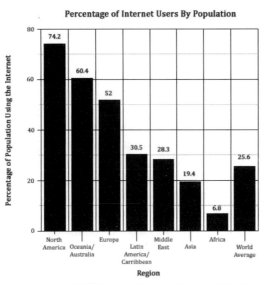

Percentage of Internet Users By Population

Internet World Stats (*www.internetworldststs.com/stat.html*)

Notice that 74 percent of Americans are on the net and there are 1.7 billion Internet users worldwide. *Every day, these numbers grow.*

I'm guessing that the number of your potential clients or followers is a lot larger than you thought! You can see from the chart that you don't have to limit yourself to spreading your message only to people in your country. All over the world, there are people who might be interested in your brand and your products. When I began writing books, it didn't occur to me that the success of my outreach would result in book tours and speaking engagements in countries as far away as South Africa, and that my writing would be translated into 14 different languages to date.

If you are eager to get started, this book lays out the crucial elements of success you'll need for the program to work. You may want to begin keeping a *Viral Explosions!* journal where you can jot down, sketch out, and expand upon your ideas. This very book started with the words "viral explosions" written in my own journal! Who knows what you'll create once you get going?

If you do have a thriving business, Website, brand, products, services, and a mailing list, I'll show you how to use them to launch your own viral explosion. If you don't, that's okay; you can create all of those at key points along the way, as I'll explain. I'll show you how to design, develop, and produce an *information-based eProduct* (which you can sell or give away in order to promote your brand or your message), write and create a landing page on the Internet, and set up partnerships with affiliates—that is, partners who can promote your products and services as part of a viral explosion. Then you can get to work on creating more products as well as building your Website traffic and increasing the number of your *e-mail subscribers.* I'll explain why an *e-mail subscriber list* of people who choose to sign up to receive information from you is a terrific vehicle for promotion, and teach you how to use it effectively.

The program in this book has been used to great success by many people, but that said, please keep in mind that I can only guide you; you're the one who decides how committed you are to launching your viral explosion. As British author Thomas Troward once said, "No writer or lecturer can convey an idea into the minds of his audience. He can only put it before them, and what they will make of it depends entirely upon themselves—assimilation is a process which no one can carry out for us." If you're ready, let's begin!

Chapter 2

Brand Yourself and Your Products and Services

What makes you and your business different? What sets you apart in the marketplace? Don't know? Don't worry—I'll help you figure it out. Before you decide what products and services you will develop and offer as part of a viral explosion, you need to create a *brand*. A brand quickly identifies for people what your expertise and style are, and it differentiates you from everyone else. A good brand conveys the essence of your business concisely and quickly and inspires buyers to check out your message and what you have to offer. It has personality, just as you do. Your brand has a strong influence on your ability to create truly special products of great value to others.

It's a fast-paced world, and people don't have time to puzzle over who you are, what you're trying to say, and what value you can bring to them. In coming up with your brand's name, don't be too cute or mysterious, and keep it simple. If you have more than one interest, and you can't easily combine them in one brand, focus on what most makes your heart sing, even if it seems there's lots of competition for a business built around that topic. Maybe the reason it's your passion is that you have a very different take or approach—that may be what allows you to quickly carve out a niche. Many people are experts on financial planning, alternative medicine, or pet care, for instance, but your personality and style may have people flocking to get advice from you regardless of how many other experts on the subject are trying to gain their attention.

I find that often people become intimidated by the idea of creating a brand. They fear there's too much competition out there, that someone else does what they do, only better, faster, cheaper, more reliably, or with more style. Don't believe it.

How many people in the world have Internet access? As of the writing of this book, the number is 1.7 billion (*www.internetworldstats.com/stats.htm*). Your job is to figure out what you can offer them, how to make them notice you and what you're promoting, and how to keep them interested in your message and your products.

It may be that you have one incredible product you want to sell via a viral explosion, and you feel you've got the expertise and credibility to do so. You may think, "I don't need a brand." But why stop with trying to sell one product? If you look closely at who you are, what you're offering, and how you came up with this particular product, you will see the seeds of a brand. If you water them, you may be able to grow a brand that will flourish, allowing you to develop even more products in the future. Once you've launched one successful viral explosion, it's easier to set off another one. You'll have established customers who have already decided they're interested in what you have to say and what you have to offer. So I hope you'll take the time to look at the bigger, long-term picture and design a brand that will work to distinguish you in the marketplace.

The Essence of a Brand

Your brand incorporates both your credibility and your style. If you've been in business for a while, you should have some idea of what makes you particularly good at what you do. As a service provider, you may be very reliable, hands-on, or innovative (note that even if you are selling products, you're ultimately providing a service, creating and delivering something of value to your customers). Your products may be unusual or customized, of exceptional value, or especially environmentally friendly. In the course of doing business day to day, it's easy to overlook what makes your business special or highly marketable. And if *you're* overlooking it, are your potential customers doing the same?

Before you start to think about "How can I turn my expertise, credibility, and style into revenue?" and envision potential products you might produce, take some time to think back to what people have said about your business and working with you (or your team). I keep a file of letters and e-mails I have from clients who've taken the time to write to me and give me feedback, so that I remember to promote the aspects of my business I might otherwise forget about. Ask your customers to tell you what they like best about your products and services. What's unusual about you? What's your specialty? What do you know, or do, that sets you apart from others?

Even if you have established a business and a brand already, it's a good idea to make sure your brand captures the core of what you do. Then, when you go to create products, you'll know how to tailor them to your brand, and what types of products will fit into your brand's offerings. An editor I know says that the best books originate in the author's personal passion, and that when authors try to chase a trend and write a book on a "hot topic" that they don't have much experience with or interest in, the book never really gels. I think that's true of businesses, too. If it's not natural for you to be edgy and modern, don't be intimidated by statistics about how large the "baby boomlet" is or feel you have to figure out their sensibility and what makes them tick in order to appeal to them. If you relate to a particular audience or demographic, and you understand their concerns, needs, and desires, you may have tremendous success selling to them and only them.

Then again, you might be surprised by who ends up buying your products and services and valuing your brand. Not everyone fits neatly into a demographer's idea of what they should be interested in. For all you know, you could have a wildly enthusiastic following in Singapore or on college campuses. You might think your core audience is salespeople and discover that entrepreneurs are your biggest customer base. Keep an open mind, but be true to yourself and what you know. Your brand should encapsulate what you have to offer.

Never build a brand by taking someone else's idea. Although it's fine to take inspiration from others, your brand should be true to who you are. Don't compare yourself to others, either. I've seen people try to distinguish themselves by saying they're a life coach trained by Joe Smith, but I don't see any reason to ride someone else's coattails and set yourself up as a sort of "B-level" Joe Smith. By all means, ask your trainer to give you a glowing endorsement for your services, but find your own brand and build your own reputation. Trust that you have something special and valuable to offer that will allow you to stand out in the marketplace. You're a unique individual. Only you can create *your* unique brand!

Start to Envision Your Brand

Your brand should include a name for your company and a style that's expressed in all of your communication with current and potential clients. The most obvious form of expression is the company name you choose, although the visual representation of your brand will matter, too.

A good brand conveys a message quickly as well as simply. A company I use to help me with finding partners for my campaigns, Hasmark Services, has a name that stands for "The **H**eart **A**nd **S**oul of **Mark**eting." "Hasmark" captures what the company delivers, and it has a logo that incorporates the shape of a heart, because "heart" is at the core of the brand.

Identify Your Credibility, Expertise, and Style

Your first goal is to figure out how to communicate your credibility and expertise to your customers. New buyers need to know what you're all about, and previous buyers need to be reminded of why they like to purchase products and services from you and not someone else.

When writing promotional copy describing your brand and your business, you'll want to include the highlights of your training or career. However, as you decide what information to include and what to leave out, imagine yourself in the position of a potential client and ask yourself, "Would I find this information helpful in making a buying decision?" The choice to purchase is often an emotional one, and credibility eases fears. If your business is new to the Internet but was established 10 years ago and you have a customer base, that helps reassure potential clients that you're not just hanging up a sign declaring yourself an expert. If you think some potential clients would feel more secure knowing something about your background or skills, or if they'd feel a personal connection to you that would cause them to extend more trust, then include that information in your promotional copy.

If you're just starting out with your business, you might not be able to point to a degree or extensive experience that validates your knowledge, or an impressive list of companies where you've given workshops, or clients who've worked with you. Everyone starts somewhere. Make a point of getting testimonials from the satisfied clients you have worked with. A few sentences of praise, testifying to the value of what you're offering, can be extremely helpful for convincing new customers to buy from you. Ask your clients if they'd be willing to provide such a testimonial (or sign off on one you've written for them), and let you use it in promotion along with their name, location, professional affiliation, and even a photograph or video of them endorsing you. The more of these pieces you have, the stronger the testimonial—at least, from the point of view of someone who doesn't know you and is looking at selling copy, a Website, or a landing page (something you'll learn more about later in the book: essentially, a landing page, also called a sales page, is a one-page, lengthy online advertisement for a product or service that has its own URL or is connected to an existing Website).

Testimonials are so important that if yours is a start-up business, you may want to exchange goods or services for a testimonial you can use in promotion. Then, too, a picture is worth a thousand words: One of my clients cleverly chose to offer free personal advice on her topic at a weekend workshop for businesswomen. She soon had a long line of people interested, and had a friend take a photograph of the crowd eagerly waiting to see her. Could you do something similar to convince your would-be customers that people are clamoring for face-time with you? Or could you use before-and-after photos that would convince your visitors that your product or service can work wonders? (Be sure to choose photos that show typical rather than exceptional results in order to be in line with FTC rules about promoting products.)

If your client is willing to give you a testimonial but isn't sure what to say, tell him what type of clients you're interested in attracting and the type of specific compliments you'd like him to include. The best testimonials are benefit-oriented: They reveal the results the person achieved after using your product or service. So, for example, your endorser might say, "Gene has an extraordinary way of explaining complex ideas in language that anyone can understand, and, as a result, I was able to launch my new business and generate immediate income." Or, "When we ran into a scheduling problem, Anna and her team were able to work around the limitations and still provide top-notch service on a tight deadline." A testimonial such as "He's great to work with" isn't as compelling as a specific, benefits-oriented testimonial such as "His patience in guiding me through the difficult task was invaluable, and he had a way of helping me weed through all the confusion and get straight to the heart of where I needed improvement. After learning from him how to better organize my time during the workday, my efficiency increased by 20 percent."

You may even suggest that your customer explain in short what her problem was before you and she worked together, and how you came to a solution. People love a personal story of suffering, struggle, and triumph. It may sound overly dramatic, but that basic, three-part story formula can be very effective for creating an emotional response in the reader, who may have a similar dilemma you can solve.

Use your testimonials on your landing page and Website. You may want to insert into the automatic signature on your e-mails a link that says "Read What Others Have Said About Our/My Service" or something similar, and which will take people to your list of endorsements. Also, ask your clients to upload their testimonials on any social networking sites you use. You can also set up your Website so that testimonial quotes appear on the front of your site—feature a list of them or have a spot where a random testimonial quote appears and is replaced by a different quote each time a visitor returns to the site.

If you want testimonials for your book, my advice is don't be afraid to dream big. Ask people if they would be willing to consider giving you a short endorsement, or write a foreword for you, and offer to send the electronic file (or a hard copy) of your manuscript, whatever is most convenient for them. Let them know what your deadline is and try to offer them plenty of time to read what you've written. You can mention the foreword or include the endorsement on the cover of the book and use it in promotional copy. If they agree, be sure to ask exactly how they'd like to be credited and make sure you follow their directions exactly.

Whenever you approach people to give you an endorsement, explain to them why they will find your product of value to people. Know their expertise, their point of view, their "philosophy," so to speak, and when you make your request, appeal to what you know matters most to them. If this expert is known for his reassuring, practical advice about losing weight naturally, don't expect him to endorse your book or teleseminar on the value of weight-loss surgery.

Define Your Brand's Style, Feel, and Look

You are at the center of your business. What is your personal style? Are you an outgoing, high-energy, flamboyant person, or would people say you're a smart, calm, sensible person who can always be counted on to identify your customer's needs quickly? These days, we're more transparent than ever before. Our personal moments can be recorded on a cell phone, turned into a photo or video file, and uploaded to a Website almost instantly. If you have an account or page on a social networking site, and have customers as friends and followers, they're getting a wider picture of you than they might have years ago. If there's a disconnect between your brand and who you are, people will notice. (Of course, you should familiarize yourself with privacy settings when using these sites for personal interactions as well.)

I remember when women were first entering the workforce in large numbers, they were very concerned about being seen as professionals. We made a point of following the strict rules of dressing that we were told must never be violated, so we all dutifully wore button earrings (never dangling ones) and floppy bow ties that served as a softer, more feminine version of the man's tie. Nowadays, we have casual Fridays, and we post on social networking sites about our personal life one minute and our business the next. Professionalism doesn't mean being strictly business at all times. It's as if we've expanded the business lunch, with shop talk and casual conversation about our daily lives mixed together, on to the Internet. If being a parent, rescuing dogs, or growing and eating organic foods is a huge part of who you are, it's going to be reflected in how you present yourself publicly. It may not be a part of your brand specifically, but people know that behind that brand is a real person who is caring, responsible, fun-loving, health conscious, and so on. Ultimately, your brand is you, but it's emphasizing your professional side.

Companies such as Zappos and Costco cultivate a corporate style that inspires intense customer loyalty. They use a new model of creating a feeling of community around their brand. People feel they could sit down with the CEOs of these companies and have a one-to-one conversation—in part because you can follow the CEOs' public posts, and they may even reply to you. The new professionalism is to be real and accessible. As a business owner, you have to strike a balance, of course. If you're constantly posting about yourself and feel you have to reply to every single person who contacts you, you're going to be working many more hours than you need to. You don't have to befriend every customer to be successful. You just have to be friendly, genuine, and reasonably accessible.

If you're somewhat reserved, that's fine; it's not going to prevent you from creating a strong brand and launching a successful viral explosion. It's up to you to determine your brand's style and just how much you share with others about who you are. The key is to be true to your personal style so that people have a feel for what they're getting when they buy from you and your company rather than from someone else.

Choose Your Brand's Name

Your brand could be your name, if you're planning on keeping your company small. There's no reason to feel you must present yourself as something you're not, and dub yourself "Robert M. Jones Enterprises International" when you're a one-person show. You might want to have two Websites: one with your brand name, and one with your name, which redirects to your brand name's site. My business is called Dynamic Destinies, Inc. and you can find it online by going to Destinies. com or to PeggyMcColl.com which will redirect you automatically to Destinies.com

If you want to use your name as your brand, you might also consider a company name such as Melinda Jones Ltd., or Terry Martin LLC, or James Roland, Inc. Be sure to talk to your accountant about the tax implications for doing business in your name versus in a company name, as there are legal differences between these different labels. Or, you might come up with a moniker based on your name. I have a metaphysical intuitive client who calls herself "Amazing Di." I've noticed that increasingly, therapists and even medical doctors who are trying to establish a brand are using "Dr." and their first name, a la Dr. Phil or Dr. Ruth (of course, you should actually have a doctorate degree, whether an MD, PhD, or other, if you use "Dr."). Would Famous Amos's or Mrs. Fields's cookies have been as desirable without those names as part of the brand? Apparently not, because when these companies were sold to major corporations, they kept the folksy brand names.

Perhaps you want to come up with a brand name that is catchy and refers to the types of products and services you offer, and the benefits for your customers. Brand names, similar to product names, or book, lecture, or workshop titles, should be short, no more than a few words, in order to be memorable and prevent typos when someone types in your domain name. You may have noticed, for example, that you can reach Barnes & Noble's online bookstore by typing in barnesandnoble.com or the simpler bn.com. Think about whether you can shorten your brand name for your Website address.

If you don't yet have a brand, brainstorm ideas with others, and think about it while you're on a long drive on an almost deserted highway, or while talking a long walk or even a long bath or shower. Then jot your ideas in a notebook and come back later to play with the possibilities. Your first try may not be quite right, but if you think more about the phrase you came up with, it may transform into something better.

Ask friends and family their thoughts. You might be surprised by the terrific ideas your friend or brother-in-law might come up with for you. That said, you are the expert. When I was first considering brand names, someone told me "Dynamic Destinies" sounded like a travel agency, but I felt that it was the right name for my business.

When thinking up combinations of words, consider using words that contain the same sound, such as Mannered Mutts, The Polite Pooch, and Polite Puppies (I'm afraid all of these have been taken, but you get the idea!). You might go with a family name (think Disney, McDonald's) or an abbreviation (think HSBC, or KFC, which changed its brand from "Kentucky Fried Chicken" to de-emphasize fact that much of their chicken is fried). Do you want brand to sound friendly, elegant, down-home, or cutting-edge? A good brand name might include an interesting contrast, such as "the Frugal Gourmet" or "the Uber Chic for Cheap blog." Or, it could be a straightforward promise or goal that people reach for, such as Best Buy, or the Get Known in the Media blog.

Another trick is to take a keyword that you want to use and do a Google image search for it, or type it into the search feature on a stock photo Website such as istockphoto.com Some of the images that come up may help you think of similar words, or images that summarize the idea. For instance, the word "frugal" may bring up photographs of piggy banks, whereas "reliability" may bring up images of arrows in the center of a bull's eye, a steel chain, and two hands shaking. The images you find might inspire words or phrases and your logo or graphics. Consult a slang dictionary (available online and in libraries) for sayings you could use or alter slightly to create an interesting play on words.

Once you feel you've come up with a strong brand name, find out whether there's a site with a very similar name that might be confused with yours. Type the brand name you're considering into a major search engine such as Google and a major online bookstore's site search, and see if someone's using a variation on it as a domain name. Could this business or site be easily confused with yours? If someone is already using the term you want to use, do you really want to compete with their brand, or can you do a little more brainstorming and come up with another idea?

A word on trademarks: I feel they're not important unless you're planning to launch a major brand, as Mark Victor Hansen and Jack Canfield did when they envisioned an entire series of Chicken Soup for the Soul ® books. A trademark has to be registered *and* patrolled; that is, every single time someone else uses your trademarked term, you must send them a cease-and-desist letter and keep a copy to prove that you're protecting your trademark. It's easy for The Xerox Corporation or Coca-Cola to hire people to scan books, blogs, newspapers, and Websites for any misuse of their trademark, but extremely difficult for a small company or an entrepreneur to do this. However, quite often, this isn't a problem, because few people want their brand confused with someone else's. So, if you've established yourself with Alicia's Ecofriendly Knits, it's very unlikely that someone else would name their business the same thing or something too similar, such as "Miranda's Ecofriendly Knits."

Settle On Your Brand's Look...and Your Look

Part of your brand is its look, which should be consistent on your Website, business cards, correspondence, product packaging, and in any promotional materials you create (You'll learn more about designing a Website later in the book, and keep in mind that to launch your first viral explosion, you don't absolutely have to have a Website, although you may need to design some packaging that contains graphics.) Your brand's look should suit your personality and style. One site I particularly love is earthy, masculine, and elegant, which reflects the personal style of the man it represents, but that look wouldn't work at all for me and my business. It's important not to let someone talk you into a look that doesn't feel right for you or that is in conflict with the core essence of your brand.

If you're not a visually oriented person, ask someone who is to help you come up with colors, images, and ideas for how to present your brand visually. A stroll through a design store or catalogue, or a bookstore with that person may help you zero in on what sort of look you want. A great Website designer will have a feel for what sort of typeface you should use, whereas you may not even notice such details. He or she should also be able to guide you on any photographs or drawings you might use, colors, and overall look. Because you want consistency in your promotional materials, put some time and thought into choosing them.

Stock photography, and even stock video and animation, is more readily available than ever. You can actually buy book jacket designs online, and hire freelancers through freelancers' Websites to come up with a logo or Website graphics. I recommend that you start by looking at what catches *your* eye. Notice what colors, typefaces, and graphics you prefer. Spend some time looking at other people's Websites—not just those in your own field, but any Websites you use and enjoy. What makes them so easy to use, so visually attractive to you?

If you are the "face" of your brand, find a photographer, hairstylist, and perhaps a makeup artist or image consultant to help you create the best photo of yourself possible. You don't have to spend a lot of money; you might be surprised at who will lend you their talents in exchange for credit (such as "Photograph by Beth Kline" run next to your photo every time you use it) and visibility. Recently, I did a book launch that attracted hundreds of people and the press, and a local jeweler asked if I would wear some of her jewelry, at no cost to me, at the event. It was a smart idea, because people did ask about my necklace in particular, including a reporter who ended up doing a story on this woman's jewelry line!

If you're not happy with the way you look, all the more reason to hire professionals to make you look good. Frankly, if you're well rested, you drink a lot of water, limit your stress, and have your photograph taken outside where the light is usually more forgiving, you might be surprised by how good you look in that photograph compared to a flash snapshot taken of you on a busy day by a friend or family member who doesn't know the tricks of making people look better in a photo.

The rules for a professional photograph are fairly simple: Choose timeless, simple clothing, hairstyles, and jewelry so that the photo doesn't look dated quickly. Work with someone who can "style" you as the photos are being taken, for instance, if a lock of hair falls out of place or your collar is sticking up. If you wear glasses, be careful about the flash and where you place the lights to prevent glare. Get a high-resolution photograph so that it has the highest quality when it's reduced to a smaller size. Take a lot of photographs, and change positions, expressions, and possibly even outfits.

Embrace Your Uniqueness!

Very often, I find that people feel they have to be completely different; that is, one-of-a-kind, nothing like anyone else in business today. What sets people apart isn't necessarily that their business is completely different from anyone else's but that there's something distinct about them, something exceptional, that is of great value to others. They are what makes their brand unique.

My client, "Amazing Di," as I mentioned before, is an intuitive counselor. Some might call her a psychic or a medium, but she told me that she didn't feel comfortable with those terms. She asked me to help her create a brand for herself, and to start, I asked her exactly what her service involves. She told me that when she sits with a client, she receives auditory messages and feels sensations in her body that help guide her in interpreting the messages she's receiving and what they might mean for that person. At the same time, she suggests how the client might use the information.

I said, "Then you're both intuitive and a counselor."

"I know," said Diane, "But I feel I shouldn't call myself an intuitive counselor because everyone who does the kind of work I do calls themselves that. I did a Google search for 'intuitive counselor' and there were so many hits, I figured I'd better come up with a really unusual way of describing myself."

I thought, "Now here's someone with what seems to me a *very* unusual service, but she's thinking she isn't unique enough!" She is one of a kind and I'm sure that her counseling sessions are distinct from the sessions you'd receive from any other intuitive counselor.

In my own circle, I know probably five real estate agents. Two of them are married to each other. Apparently, there are enough properties to buy and sell in the Ottawa area to support so many real estate agents that I know five of them myself, and they're doing quite well from what I can tell. Being "totally different from everyone else" isn't what's needed so much as setting yourself apart through your quality, excellence, and style.

It may take some time to find your own niche that allows you to stand out, but niches often carve themselves. You begin working with a certain type of customer, he spreads the word about you to his colleagues and peers, and before you know it, you've specialized in serving a particular clientele. Then, you can branch out from there and start thinking about what other clients you'd like to work with. If you have a good brand name and look, you should be able to attract a wide variety of customers.

Busting the Myths About Internet Marketing

Once you have your brand, I know you can launch a successful viral explosion, so I hope you'll let go of any misconceptions you might have. Here are some of the myths I've heard about Internet marketing, which I have discovered first-hand are simply that: myths.

Myth: There's too much competition for me to make money with Internet marketing.

Reality: You may have competitors, but not everyone will care as deeply as you do about providing quality and value. The people who achieve the greatest success are always willing to grow, learn, and adjust to their clients' needs. They're ahead of the pack, and they're delivering what people need and desire. The competitor you're concerned about may not get a lot of traffic to its Website, and the owners may not be marketing it or doing any sort of outreach. Some sites are static, and have been around for quite some time with the same information on them, so people don't come back to them and discover that they're offering products. They may have poor-quality items, poor customer service, or any number of problems that your company won't have.

You can find your own niche and make money. You don't have to be Coke or Pepsi, one of the big established brands, to find an audience of loyal customers. You might brew a specialty cola that people all over the country or even the world simply *must* have. When you see your niche forming, embrace it.

Myth: You must have an established Website in order to make money using Internet marketing.

Reality: Although it's great to have a Website and a good-sized e-mail list of people who have already expressed interest in your brand, you can simply create a strong landing page, also known as a sales page, and work with affiliates who will promote your offering to the people on their own e-mail list.

Myth: You have to be an excellent copywriter to create effective promotional materials.

Reality: You can hire someone or use a template. Or you can do it yourself, following successful examples (more on this in Chapter 9).

Myth: You have to have excellent technical skills to make money on the Internet.

Reality: Much of the Web is user-friendly, and technology that allows you do perform a wide variety of tasks is often quite cheap and easily available—and the situation is only getting better. New software and applications are released all the time, and you can very often find personalized help with a few keystrokes. Type your technology problem into a search engine and you're very likely to find a forum that answers it right away. I'm not technologically inclined, but I've launched many viral explosions. I've listed in the Resources section some of the sites I've used to help me.

Myth: You have to have a large list of clients and fans for your brand if you want to launch a successful viral explosion.

Reality: You don't need to have a list of subscribers and clients as long as you team up with others who have lists (although if you do have a list of your own, all the better. In Chapter 7, you'll learn how to assemble one).

Myth: You have to manufacture something to create a viral explosion.

Reality: We live in the Information Age. Information-based products such as eCourses, Webinars, teleseminars, and eBooks can deliver value without your having to manufacture anything.

Myth: You have to invest a lot of time and money to create a viral explosion.

Reality: People have seen a great return on their investment after as little as 50 hours' work and several hundred dollars spent creating their landing page and products. Thanks to technology, production costs can be minimal, and you may be able to deliver your product electronically, saving packaging, shipping, and handling costs.

When you create a viral explosion for a teleseminar, eBook, or other eProduct that does not require production costs, you might be surprised at how little money you have to invest initially. You can write your own landing page based on a free template downloaded from the Internet. I just created a viral explosion for a product called *Relax Your Way to Wealth* and it cost me $4.99 to reserve the domain name and $7.99 a year to host the landing page. I used the free template available from my *hosting service*, had a copywriter write up the copy for me, which he was able to do in a few days, and plugged that copy into the template. Then I launched a viral explosion and watched as sales poured in. I've known people who designed their own Websites using software from their hosting company, or paid a few hundred dollars to a Website designer, and ended up with a very professional-looking site. Shopping-cart software that allows you to collect money securely, and pay your affiliates commissions (which you'll learn about in Chapter 6), is inexpensive as well.

Creating a viral explosion is like creating a business: It requires an initial investment of time and money, but you'll see a return, especially if you use a viral explosion along with other tools for expanding your brand's visibility in the marketplace.

Your business will grow, expand, contract, and change with time. Ideally, your brand name is one you can live with for a while, one that doesn't feel too trendy—unless, of course, "trendiness" is core to your brand! Consider your brand carefully and choose one that feels right for you.

Then, once you are clear on who you are and what qualities you bring to your products and services, and how you want to present yourself and your business, you're ready to conceive of the specific products and services you want to sell. Get ready to be creative, because there are many possibilities I'll bet you haven't even imagined.

Chapter 3

Discover a Need You Can Fill

Never lose track of this very important truth:

It's not what you want to offer that matters, it's what your customer is interested in.

If you believe that you've got something to offer that others will value and desire, and even pay for, then you can create products and services that are true to your brand and can be the centerpiece of your viral explosion. The question you must ask yourself is, "How can I build my brand and business, make some money, *and* provide service and something of value to others?" *The point of marketing is to match up what you have to offer with customers who are interested in what you have and willing to act on that interest.*

There's a common myth that online marketing is totally different from offline marketing. That's simply not true. In fact, the basic formula I just provided you—match your expertise with a product that fills a need in the marketplace—has proven to be a winner for all sorts of products and services—offline and online. The problem is that too many people find a need in the market-place but don't consider whether they have or can achieve the credibility or expertise to create the appropriate product or service to fill that need. Alternately, they have expertise and credibility, but they create a product without considering whether it fills a need.

You've already learned how to identify your credibility and style to create a brand. Next, you need to start looking at opportunities in the marketplace so that you can come up with products and services you can create and deliver that will plug into people's needs.

What Are People Thinking About?

Your current customers are a terrific source of informa-tion about needs in the marketplace, but you might also look at what people everywhere are thinking and talking about. What's on the minds of your friends, neighbors, and acquain-tances lately? Is there a common mood these days? What are people dealing with, thinking about, or yearning for? Remember, the Web offers you access to people around the world. Your topic may be of great interest to others you can reach via an Internet viral explosion.

As I write this, the economy is not doing well. What sorts of needs, emotional and practical, does that generate? Some people respond to a poor economy by becoming more frugal and cost-conscious. They're looking for bargains and guid-ance on how to stretch their money. Some people respond to an economic downturn by taking bigger risks. They want to follow their hearts instead of playing it safe in a job they're not happy in. They're in the mood for products and services that appeal to the dreams they've been ignoring for years. How can your expertise and knowledge benefit them at a time like this?

Listen to what your neighbors, teenagers, and relatives are talking about and thinking about, and get ideas for products and services they'd be interested in. Notice what people are buying or using, and ask yourself, "How can I meet the needs of the people who are drawn to social networking to get in touch with old friends, people who want to buy vegetables in bulk from local farmers, or investors who want to pick up real estate bargains in a down economy?" Find the needs and start thinking about how you can meet them.

One neat trick for finding out what people are saying about your topic of expertise or your type of products, and what they're looking for, is to type a name or description into a search engine or the search function on a social networking site. You might discover that there are people clamoring for "custom sweaters," a product you provide, but they want them but for their dogs, not themselves! Maybe the buzzword in parenting today is "good enough" (okay, that's actually two words, but you get the idea). What need is causing people to flock to a site called *BadMommy.com*? I wouldn't be attracted to such a site, but if mothers are feeling anxious about the pressure to be a perfect mom, can you meet their needs for confidence and reassurance?

Gary Vaynerchuk, whose online video blog, Wine Library TV, has become extremely popular on the Web, is an example of how one person can join the many conversations online about a particular topic and build his brand by meeting a particular need—in his case, the need for information about wines delivered in an entertaining way. No one sells wine quite like Gary Vaynerchuk does, with his down-to-earth presentation style, colorful language, and sports-team spit bucket. His entertaining video blog got many people excited about his brand, and he helped spread the word through social media sites and an e-mail subscriber list that kept people coming back to his site to see his latest video blog and order some wine.

Remember to look at new technologies for ideas on new needs or longings people have as a result of changes in their lives. Every time a new technology comes along, it presents new opportunities. I know a gentleman who offered a course through the local recreation department for people who wanted to learn how to use all the bells and whistles on their cell phones. He was able to give the class an overview of all the potential in those phones they owned, and personalized guidance on how to instant-message, download a ringtone, and reconnect with the person whose call they'd just missed. All of this built interest in his cell phone store located nearby and the products he has to offer. He might also decide to teach people over the Internet.

Diane Craig, an image consultant who realized she could expand her market and reach people anywhere in the world, sought me out for advice. She wanted to expand her market outside of Toronto, where she lives, without having to travel extensively. After she learned about the information-based products she could create, and the way viral explosions work, she realized she wasn't limited to selling to local people. She decided to create a teleseminar that could be attended by anyone who had a phone and Internet access. She would create visual images, including graphics and photos, that clearly demonstrated her message, and which customers were able to access on the Internet and download to look at while she was giving her presentation on the phone. In this way, she could reach clients who could benefit from her wisdom, knowledge, and guidance without having to be in the same physical location as they were. How might you adapt your one-on-one services to people who are sitting by their computer in Peoria, Illinois, or a rural area in Scandinavia or Ireland?

Learning From Previous Customers

If you already have clients, offline or online, and at least one product or service, consider them an important source of information and feedback. They may even be able to tell you what your next product should be, or which of your services they find the most valuable, which can help you decide on the one to sell via an Internet viral explosion. To stay in contact with your clients and learn from them:

~ *Offer them a regular newsletter with a contact link.* In your newsletters, encourage them to contact you with any questions, suggestions, or comments.

~ *Blog, and encourage them to post a reply.* You might end your blog pieces by asking them to share their thoughts and experiences; for example, "Have you had a similar experience?" or "What would you do in this situation?"

~ *Have an online forum on your Website.* Your customers and followers can interact with you and each other and create a community.

~ *Communicate with your customers using social media.* Post a question to get them talking to you and each other.

~ *Have a "contact" section on your Website.* Make it easy for them to e-mail you via their e-mail software or a feedback form.

~ *Do in-person presentations.* It's helpful to physically meet your customers and chat with them.

~ *When delivering teleseminars open up the call for questions.* Be sure to tell them you'd like to hear their stories as well, because these can serve as helpful examples to the other participants, and allow you to give your take on their story.

~ *E-mail your teleseminar or Webinar students an evaluation form.* Include a question about whether they could use help in some area that the teleseminar or Webinar didn't cover.

When you're in touch with your customers, you might ask them, "If I were to create a new service, what would you suggest?" or "Is there any product that would help you make the most of my services?" Pay attention to their questions for you. What do they seem to need: information, products, services, advice and guidance, validation, encouragement, inspiration? They may need or desire something tangible, like a workbook that helps them stay on track when using the program you offer them, or something emotional, such as one-to-one encouragement when they're feeling overwhelmed or insecure. Can you create a product or service that meets those needs?

Query your customers on how they're enjoying what you've sold them in the past. Ask them if it's been of value, and if so, why. Notice if they've found an unusual use you hadn't thought of, and ask them about it. If they use your product differently when they travel, think about offering a travel version. If they are using what you've taught them about office management when coaching their child's sports team, consider whether you could create a product that has that particular spin on your information.

Sometimes, your customers appreciate your product so much that they want more from you. The feedback I received for my book *Your Destiny Switch: Master Your Key Emotions and Attract the Life of Your Dreams* was that many readers wanted even more guidance on dealing with fear and transforming it into faith. I took what I'd written on fear, expanded on it, and created a double CD called *Turn Fear Into Faith.* In fact, authors often tell me that the idea for their second book comes out of a chapter in their first book that they had a hard time keeping to a typical chapter length because there was so much to say on the subject.

Sometimes, strange as it may seem, some potential customers would want *less* information and detail rather than more. You may have created an information-based product of great value, such as a book or a class taught in person or on the Internet or phone, that is chock-full of helpful advice. but some people need to receive that information in smaller, more digestible pieces. Let's say my *Magnet for Money* 6-CD set was selling great but I kept hearing from potential customers that they didn't have the time to invest in such a substantial program. I could decide to create a shorter version, or offer a subscription service so that they could receive a weekly e-mail with a valuable nugget of information from the program. There's a successful service that allows people to receive entire books broken into small excerpts, sent sequentially at a time of day that the customer specifies. The idea is that some people will read their e-mail on their computer or smart phone fairly consistently, but will rarely pick up a book. Using a subscription service that breaks up the information into small pieces delivered by e-mail, they discipline themselves to read a large block of text that they wouldn't otherwise. Now, I would simply purchase the book and make certain I read it, but that's me. Other people operate differently. Think about how you might break down your information into smaller chunks that people can receive in a convenient form.

You can repurpose your material by changing the form of delivery or combining several products or services into one package. I've found that often people desire a large package of information and materials because it represents a commitment to their goal. If they need to lose weight, they probably want more than a book that tells them what to eat and how to set up an exercise program. Weight Watchers is highly successful because they know people want personalized guidance from someone who has successfully lost weight and kept it off using their program, a support group that meets in person or online, a way of tracking what they've eaten, and easy access to recipes. Think about all the many ways you could serve your customers, and offer them a variety of options that meet their practical needs as well as their emotional needs.

Not Just a Need but an Urgent Need!

The more urgent the need you're fulfilling, the better your chances of launching a highly successful viral explosion. One way an urgent need is created is if the supply can't meet the demand. As I write this, people who know how to use social media effectively to generate profits are in high demand because there's a shortage of experts and a great need for guidance in this area. Often, I see people spend a lot of time or money trying to boost their visibility on these sites but not having a clear sense of how to turn their efforts into profits. Those who have good, solid ideas and formulas can make money like never before. As with any niche, the social media experts who will stand out are the ones who offer something a little different from what everyone else is selling and who know how to get results. I believe that the experts, entrepreneurs, and businesspeople who deeply care about their clients and are committed to providing top-quality service, going above and beyond what others provide, are the ones whose brands will not only survive but thrive.

At any given point, there's an urgent practical need for certain products and services, but there are also practical needs that will always exist, which you might be able to fulfill in your own way with your products and services. People will always look for advice and help with:

~ Career success.
~ Business success.
~ Finances.

~ Finding romance.

~ Creating and maintaining good relationships.

~ Parenting.

~ Health and fitness.

~ Emotional well-being.

These needs can feel quite urgent to people. If you don't believe me, just look at how many books, Websites, products, and services are tailored to the bride who wants the perfect wedding that will meet her need for romance, or to the person who wants to have a fit, toned, healthy body.

It's possible that, on closer look, the potential product or service that first comes to your mind isn't one that people strongly need. However, you might design it in such a way that people feel they absolutely *have* to have it.

In general, people are highly motivated by their emotions. When they're fearful, they want to feel reassured. When they're sad or lethargic, they want to be uplifted, energized, and inspired. When they're overwhelmed, they want to believe there's someone who or something that can rescue them and solve their problems. It may seem that your client is buying a CD set, teleseminar, or book on how to make money refurbishing preowned vehicles, but what he's also buying is hope that he can turn junk into cash and make enough money to get out of that dead-end job that's been driving him crazy and get his kids into a good private school. The authors that take my course on "How to Be a Best-Selling Author" don't just want to publish their book so some people can benefit from the knowledge contained in its pages. They long to see their name on a best-seller list and feel the intense pride that comes from being able to refer to themselves as a "best-selling author." The word "best-seller" speaks to people's dreams and deepest longings.

As you consider your potential product, think about what its emotional appeal is. Which of these emotional benefits will your buyer experience?

reassurance	joy
a sense of safety	courage
amusement	hope
faith	a sense of contribution
wonderment	empowerment
tranquility	self-acceptance
relief	emotional connection to others
pride	a sense of purpose
self-worth	a sense of importance
fulfillment	inspiration

Take your time as you go through this list. Then, when you've identified some of the emotional benefits, find the one or two that you feel may be most important to your potential customers. How might you turn up the volume on those benefits and give your clients an even stronger sense of amusement, faith, relief, pride, and so on, so that they feel an even greater need for your product? Be sure the emotional benefits you're offering are exciting and powerful.

When I created my *Magnet for Money* 6-CD program, I saw people struggling with changing their relationship to money and their finances, and I knew they were very eager to solve their financial problems. They needed to build their confidence and faith as much as they needed solid techniques for building wealth. Rather than simply give them strategies, which was their practical need, I wanted to help them see that they actually knew more about making, attracting, and managing money than they gave themselves credit for. I decided to do a seminar with open Q&A sessions after each component so I could speak to them directly about that specific topic. I encouraged participants to tell me about a time when they'd found success using a technique, and helped them to remember what had worked for them in the past. By choosing this format, I was able to offer them the benefit of my expertise in this area, which solved their problem of not knowing what to do to attract more money into their lives. But it also allowed me to provide them with the emotional benefits of feeling validated and supported, as well as part of a community of people who share the same challenges.

Look to the Past

One more way to get ideas is to look back to the past and see if you can resurrect a product or service that was left by the wayside. This may be a product you created that you can revamp and update. Or, it may be something that someone else used to offer that you can spin in your own way and sell via a viral explosion.

Not long ago, someone pointed out to me an Internet site where you can order the candies from your childhood like Snaps licorice and candy necklaces. These items may not be big money-makers for your local chain drugstores, but clearly there's still a market for them. Some sites offer manual typewriters and cast-iron dinner bells as well as other old-fashioned items. There's even been an increase in sales of vinyl records lately. I'm old enough to remember when the hot new music format was the 8-track tape, then the cassette, the CD, and audio downloads. To me, vinyl records are big, heavy, and difficult to store properly, but the music on vinyl records sounds different from that in other formats, and for some music lovers, that means a lot. Also, kids who grew up with personal music players are discovering the joy of playing music that fills the room and that is shared with friends who are listening along with you.

There's a saying that "everything old is new again," so I like to revisit past products and services now and again to see if there's anything I might alter a bit and offer once more. Currently, I'm taking a product I created called GoalMAPs, which I designed in the 1990s and used with corporate teams I worked with, and revising it to be used by individuals. I'll create a teleseminar and, most likely, other related products around this idea that still has value and that has helped me immensely in my personal and business goals.

What "old-fashioned" products or services might you offer? Many people no longer have skills such as cooking from scratch, gardening, sewing, knitting, writing with good penmanship, and so on. As an exercise, ask yourself the following four questions:

1. *In my field of interest, what technique or strategy did I use a long time ago that would be valuable to today's market?* You may have created a checklist for use with a particular client years ago and now you realize that you could revise it slightly to use with new clients.

2. *Is there a product or service that used to be readily available and is hard to find now, that some people wish was available again?* Vinyl records and manual typewriters are examples of products some people wish they could have today despite the ready availability of audio files and word processing programs.

3. *How could I update the old products and services I and others once loved?* Perhaps a new generation would appreciate the humorous writing you did years ago and could now update and incorporate into a blog or an eBook.

4. *Can I use new technologies to provide a service that's a perennial favorite?* Whereas before, you had to be in the same room with someone to ensure that you could both look at the same computer screen, now you can do it remotely. Does this offer you possibilities for training someone who lives in a different city from yours?

~~~

Now that you have a good sense of how to match up your brand with eager customers, let's look more closely at information-based products you can put together and offer as part of a viral explosion. Many of these products require a minimal financial investment and can be stored and delivered using technology rather than a warehouse (or dining room!) and a mailing service. Later in the book, you'll learn the specifics of how to produce them, design a launch, and set off your own viral explosion.

Chapter 4
Information-Based Products You Can Sell or Give Away

I believe you can sell anything on the Internet, whether it's bananas or widgets. Take a look at some of the crazy items that have sold on eBay! A fellow from Nebraska even auctioned off advertising space on his forehead!

But more than ever before, we live in an age of information. People often feel overwhelmed by how much there is to learn and know, yet they recognize that information can be the key to solving their problems and living the life they desire. If you have a passion—not just a mere interest, but a passion—you develop expertise and credibility through time as you pursue that passion. Your body of knowledge is of value to others, and you can create and distribute information-based products to your customers quickly, and, in some cases, for very little financial investment. My personal passions are self-growth and Internet marketing, and I've created many products based in those passions and used them to launch successful viral explosions.

Some people give away their information free to who-ever asks, perhaps in the hope of selling something to that person later on. That's great, and it can be an effective way to build interest in their brand, drive traffic to their Website, and increase the size of their subscriber list. Many people have raised their visibility on the Internet by providing free information to others, not just on their Website but through information-based products they've given away. However, as you think about the body of knowledge and the wisdom you've gained in pursuing your passion, and its value, imagine how you might profit from all that knowledge, too, and funnel the revenue back into building your brand and getting out your message. In this chapter, you'll learn the basics about the most common information-based products and be able to start envisioning which ones you'd like to develop:

~ Downloadable audio files.

~ Downloadable video files.

~ CDs or DVDs.

~ Teleseminars.

~ Webinars.

~ eBooks.

~ Books.

~ eCourses.

~ Mentoring, coaching, and consulting programs.

~ Monthly subscription services.

Of course, as I've said before, you can sell other products as well, and if you've already got a tangible product you're promoting, think about how an information-based eProduct that you give away or sell might drive the sales of that product you're already offering.

Let's look at each of the types of information-based products in detail so you can start envisioning which formats would work best for you.

Audio and Video Downloads

Audio and video files can be downloaded, uploaded, and exchanged electronically, making them an excellent vehicle for getting your message out or providing information to people. You might want to offer people an audio recording of a live presentation you made or interview you conducted with another expert or a panel of experts. You could also create an audio download of a teleseminar you hosted previously, and a video download of a Webinar that you recorded when you presented it. Or, you can create an informational audio that you later use as the basis of an eBook.

Videos can be created using Web cameras (many computers now come with them built in) or video equipment. High-resolution digital cameras have come down in price considerably, and you could even use a flip camera to shoot film digitally, then transfer it to your computer to edit it.

Although people often love information provided in video form, especially if it has a high entertainment value, it does take up a lot of space in your hard drive, and because they're big files, videos can take a long time to transfer, too. They can also take up a lot of bandwidth on your Website if you offer it for download, and some Website hosting companies will charge you more money if you need a lot of bandwidth. However, videos do not have to be downloaded to be viewed. So as long as you're only offering *streaming* video, which means that the video plays without downloading, bandwidth will not be a problem. By all means, allow people to access video on your site, but if you want your video to go viral, post your video on video sharing sites.

Note, too, that videos can also be embedded into Microsoft PowerPoint presentations, loaded onto Websites, and posted on social networking sites—or pressed onto DVDs.

CD or DVD Products

You can burn audio information onto CDs or DVDs, and burn videos onto DVDs. Unlike with audio and video downloads, you'll have to invest in packaging for the actual product before you do your viral explosion (although the outlay will be reimbursed if you sell enough products to make back your investment). With any CD or DVD product, you'll also have to keep a good-sized stash of the product and mailing supplies in your home, or you can make arrangements to have a *fulfillment house*, a company that offers storage and other services for business owners, take care of the orders for you, and pay them when an order is placed.

The advantage to having video and audio files on CDs and DVDs is that many people find a physical disk easier to work with than an electronic file, and may not have the latest technology for quality listening and viewing of electronic files. Also, you can sell CDs and DVDs, in packages, at in-person events such as lectures and workshops. Plus, it can be extremely satisfying to hold in your hands a physical product that you create; there's a sense of completion and ownership that's not always so strong with an electronic product.

Audio and Video Downloads: Pros	Audio and Video Downloads: Cons
Low cost to produce.	Must learn the appropriate software or work with someone who knows how to use it.
No packaging costs.	No physical product.

Can transmit without any shipping costs.	Video files are very big and can be difficult to transmit, and they take up a lot of storage space on your Website and hard drive.
Can be sold at in-person events if you convert the product to a CD or DVD.	Takes time and money to convert product to a physical product.
Can be uploaded and stored online, freeing up disk space on your hard drive.	

CDs and DVDs: Pros	CDs and DVDs: Cons
Having a physical product rather than an electronic one may offer you some emotional benefits.	Somewhat more costly to produce than an audio or digital file.
Can easily sell at in-person events.	Must create packaging which costs money, and find a place to store the products if you keep several on hand.
	Could end up stocking product you don't sell.

Teleseminars

A *teleseminar* is a **tele**phone **seminar.** The presenter secures a teleconference line through a service and has attendees dial in at a predetermined time to participate in this live event. As the moderator, the presenter controls the call. She decides when the attendees can be heard and when they're silenced, which allows her to present her material uninter-rupted on a line with no background noise (such as people coughing, having conversations with their kids in the other room, running water, and so on). Then she can open up the line for questions and answers if desired.

Teleseminars are surprisingly economical ways to get your information directly to your customers and receive feed-back from them. You can order a service for free, or a small monthly fee and typically you're allowed as many as 150 lines for attendees and can host unlimited teleseminars (if you'd like to access more than 150 lines, they typically charge you a little more). The more callers you have, however, the more difficult it is to manage a live Q&A session. If I have a very large group of students for a teleseminar, I will often ask them to log on to the Internet and e-mail me their questions, which I'll read aloud and answer for the benefit of all. Otherwise, I'll open up the line for Q&A and anyone can speak up.

You might be surprised at how many people from out of the country are interested in attending your seminar. Because the participants will be calling in to the teleconference phone line, it's best if they have an unlimited calling package, with no long distance charges, or use a *voiceover internet (v.i.) protocol* such as Skype. Fortunately, unlimited calling packages and v.i. proto-col packages are very common nowadays. I've done many tele-seminars and never received an objection to the format from someone who would have had to pay long distance charges.

I like teleseminars because you can do a multimedia pre-sentation as long as your participants have Internet access so they can download any files they'll need for the class and access the recording afterward. For the 8-hour teleseminar this book is based on, I created an eBook that served as a workbook. I also created a PowerPoint presentation that attendees could download and look at while I was speaking. My PowerPoint presentation included links so that people could instantly access the Websites I was talking about. However, I also incorporated screen shots from Websites that were no longer available. If I'd wanted to, I could have inserted a video into the Power Point presentation as well. Because videos are big files that can take a lot of time to download, I would probably instead insert into the presentation a link to a video uploaded onto a video sharing site so that people can watch it without having to download it! So, although the simplest form of a teleseminar is purely auditory, you can combine it with documents, eBooks, Excel spreadsheets, and PowerPoint presentations that your attendees access through a secured Website and provide a visual element as well.

Some people don't like teleseminars because they prefer to take in information visually rather than auditorily. Of course, if you use multimedia elements, this might not be a problem for them.

Another great thing about teleseminars is that they are easy to set up. If you do public speaking on your topic, there's a lot of preparation and travel involved. Even if you've delivered the same lecture or workshop before, you have to decide what to wear and how you're going to get to the venue, you have to make photocopies of handouts and figure out how many to bring, check the weather reports and road conditions to be sure you can get there on time, make arrangements for childcare while you're gone, and so on. A teleseminar eliminates all of that work for you. You could do a teleseminar in your fuzzy slippers and bathrobe, while sitting with your laptop in your backyard if you wanted. Your attendees can access all the "handouts" online and download them before class begins.

Webinars

Webinar is short for **Web**-based sem**inar.** It's a presentation, lecture, or workshop that's transmitted over the Internet that allows the attendee to see the presenter, and any of her presentation materials, in real time.

At present, Webinars can cost more to host than teleseminars do because you either pay the service a fee based on the length of your presentation and the number of visitors, or you pay a higher monthly fee for unlimited than you would with teleseminars. Also, with most service providers, you can't have as many attendees as you can with teleseminars, although prices may come down in the future as more companies get into the business of selling Webinar services.

However, one advantage Webinars have over teleseminars is that they're visual and allow people to view you in real time. They can take the place of an in-person lecture, and allow viewers to see your facial expressions and body language. This is especially helpful if you're demonstrating an activity or how to use a product.

As with teleseminars, you have extra features available to you that can enhance your presentation. You might switch the Webinar into Internet mode so that you can have your attendees watch in real time as you show them Websites. You can switch to a PowerPoint presentation or a visual whiteboard, either of which allows you to point out specific areas on screen or demonstrate what you're talking about. Webinars also feature a chat function so that people can make comments or ask questions during your presentation.

A Webinar, just like a teleseminar, can also be accessed later if it's archived on a Website. Generally, once you've archived the webinar or teleseminar and made it available for downloading, you charge less money than you would charge for the original live event, because purchasers of the archived seminar aren't able to participate in the Q&A session or ask you questions in real time.

Teleseminars: Pros	Teleseminars: Cons
Unlike with a live lecture, you can present to hundreds or even thousands of people without having to leave your home, which is very convenient!	No physical or eye contact with your attendees; no one can see your facial expressions or body language.
Can do demonstrations using multimedia such as video embedded in a PowerPoint presentation.	Audience needs to know how to call in, download, and work with the software you're using such as PowerPoint.
Easy to set up and run.	Unlike with Webinars, you must be crystal-clear with your instructions to attendees when referring to materials in other media that are part of the class, because they're not looking at the same screen you are.

Webinars: Pros	Webinars: Cons
Easy to set up and run.	A little more complicated than hosting a teleseminar.
Inexpensive.	A little more expensive than a teleseminar.
Can demonstrate activities, make eye contact, or have audience see your body language.	Can't physically touch audience as you could at a live event (shake hands, hug, and so on.)
Unlike with a teleseminar, you can do visual demonstrations without using multimedia elements.	Audience needs to be able to access the Internet.

eBooks

An *eBook* is an electronic file book. Often in Adobe.pdf format, it can be transmitted electronically and read on a computer, eReader, or smart phone.

Many people like eBooks because they prefer to receive information by reading rather than by listening or viewing video. For fast readers and people skilled at skimming written material, eBooks can be a more convenient format than audio or video. Also, they can be instantly accessed; there's no driving to the bookstore or waiting for a book to arrive in the mail.

One of the advantages of an eBook is that it doesn't have the production costs of a book. There's no paper to buy and no printer to pay. The product doesn't have to be stuffed into a padded envelope and shipped because it's delivered electronically. Another advantage is that you can make it any length you choose. You can create a document that runs 20 pages or 200 pages. You have the freedom to design it any way you wish, which is not the case if you want to publish a physical book. Physical books have to be a certain length to work with the available bindings, so they are bound in signatures; that is, groups of 16 pages (which is why children's books are so often exactly 48 pages, or 3 signatures, long). With a self-published eBook or printed book, you're the one who makes all the decisions on length, and you have plenty of freedom to create it exactly as you'd like it.

Also, eBooks never run out of stock. You'll never have to tell a customer to come back later to buy it, as you might with a traditional book. What's more, because it is so easy to revise and upload, you can update eBooks as needed.

Physical Books

Do you have enough knowledge and wisdom about your subject to fill a book, or even several books? You can go the traditional route of trying to find a publisher who will create the physical book, distribute it to bookstores, and help with publicity, or you can do it all on your own.

A major distinction between a traditional publisher and a self-publishing or print-on-demand service is that with the latter, you pay a certain amount of money to receive finished books, and as long as the book is not libelous or obscene, they will print your book even if they think it's not particularly well-written or marketable. However, unlike with an eBook, when you have a physical book, whether it's self-published or one a publisher created, you get to experience the satisfaction of holding an object in your hands and saying, "I created this." I remember well the moment I first held my first book in my hands and what an awesome feeling it was. So if you're thinking about writing a book, ask yourself whether or not having a physical object would matter to you (fortunately, if your concern is having a physical object to sell at in-person events, you can easily print up a handful of copies, or even one copy, using a print-on-demand service—more on this later).

With a traditional publisher, of course, you end up with a physical book, too. However, to get a book deal, you need the approval of several people in the company, which may include other editors and representatives from the marketing, sales, or foreign rights departments.

Traditionally, book publishers invest in the books they decide to publish. They pay for the production costs, and in return for receiving the right to publish your book, a book publisher will typically pay you an advance against your future earnings on sales based on their estimate of how many copies you would sell. They also do some marketing of the book. The industry is changing rapidly, however, and some publishers are revising their rules in order to lower their risk of not earning back their investments in the books they publish. Nowadays, a traditional book publisher may not always work the "traditional" way. Advances are sometimes very low, and some publishers ask that the author commit to buying a certain number of books.

eBook: Pros	eBook: Cons
Easy for skilled readers to read and even skim.	Some people prefer not to have to read at length.
Very low production costs.	No advance against royalties like in traditional book publishing.
Can update and revise easily.	Very difficult to get the book into bookstores and other stores, even if you make physical copies via a print-on-demand service.
Don't need to have much technical skill to create it.	May need to convert the eBook into various formats for uploading to different sites, such as online bookstores.
Writing skills don't need to meet the standards of professional editors.	If you want the book edited, you must hire someone.
Total freedom in terms of length, form, writing style, and pricing.	No standard pricing formulas for eBooks as for traditional books, so you'll have to figure out what you can charge.
Easily transferred electronically, no shipping costs, can be stored in your computer's hard drive.	Not the same emotional payoff you'd have if you produced a physical book, unless you print up some copies.
Can print copies on demand using a print-on-demand service.	Must plan ahead to have physical books created via a print-on-demand service to sell at in-person events.

Traditional Book Publishing

Traditional book publishers only publish books that meet their editorial standards, and even then, they want to feel confident that they can sell enough copies to not only recoup their investment but also make a profit.

If the publishing house feels the book needs a lot of work, they may ask you to hire a freelance editor or a ghostwriter to make the book better. When I first teamed up with my literary agent, Cathy Hemming, she suggested that we find a professional writer to write the book I wanted to sell: *Your Destiny Switch*. To be honest, my feelings were a little hurt. I'd been writing my own copy for years and had written self-published books. Cathy explained to me that there's no stigma for hiring someone to write your book for you, and that book-writing is a specialized skill. To maximize my book's sales potential, she said it would be very helpful to have a professional ghostwriter who could interview me, read any text I had written, do research on some topics, and write the actual manuscript. I agreed to take this route, and was able to sell the book based on the proposal my agent and I had created before I had lined up a writer. Then, we found a writer and paid her fee out of the publisher's advance.

Part of the reason a book publisher wanted to buy the rights to *Your Destiny Switch* was not just because my ideas are absolutely awesome (smile) and promised to be a wonderful book, but because they could tell that I had a strong *platform*; that is, the ability to get the word out about my book in a big way and sell copies on my own. After all, I was an Internet marketing expert who had turned many of their own authors' books into best-sellers!

Traditional book publishers expect authors to do the vast majority of marketing for their own books, so a well-developed platform is important whether or not you have any specific marketing expertise (of course, you will after reading this book!). Let's say you're a well-known blogger with thousands of subscribers to your newsletter and a presence in social media, and someone who regularly speaks to audiences on your subject (in person or online through teleseminars and Webinars), and you have some media connections. A book publisher may judge that as a strong platform. If you're willing to invest time and money in marketing yourself, and you have some great ideas, that will help you net a book publishing deal as well.

A traditional publisher will try to distribute your book into brick-and-mortar bookstores as well as online stores, which can be a big advantage because, due to low profit margins, it's very difficult to convince brick-and-mortal bookstores to carry print-on-demand or self-published books. I hadn't realized this when I self-published my first book, *On Being...The Creator of Your Destiny*. I called up the buyer for the biggest bookstore chain in Canada and she told me that if I wanted my book carried in her chain's stores, I'd have to talk to the wholesaler and convince him to stock the book. The wholesaler would take a cut of each book sold, so when I calculated how much that would eat into my profit margin, I knew I didn't want to do it. I just didn't feel it was crucial to get my book into bookstores. But if that's a goal of yours, be aware that on your own, you'll have to sacrifice a big chunk of your profits if you need to go through a wholesaler to get bookstore distribution. (If you self-publish, you may be able to sell books into an individual bookstore or retail store—even a gift store—yourself if you approach the owner and can agree on how much of the revenue the store can keep.)

Self-Publishing and Print-on-Demand Publishing Services

An advantage of selling your books on your own, without involving a publisher, is the profit margin. The money you make per copy on a book sold by a publisher is small change compared to the money you make per copy on a self-published book, but the question is, how many copies can you sell if you self-publish? If the publisher can sell 5,000 copies with you making $1 a copy, and you can only sell 200 copies at, say, $8 profit per a copy, you'll make a lot more money selling the publisher the right to publish your book. But if you could sell 2,500 copies on your own at $8 profit per copy, that's a lot more money in your pocket.

A publisher may even be able to get you some related sales; for instance, it might sell foreign-language rights to a publisher in another country or sell audio-book rights. With self-publishing and print-on-demand services, you have to make these sales efforts on your own, or hire someone to help you, or pay for these extra services as part of your "publishing" package.

If you self-publish a book, or use a print-on-demand service, you will pay all the production costs yourself. With self-publishing, you have to commit to pay for a minimum print run of a certain number of copies. With print-on-demand, you can print as few as one or two copies of a book at a time instead of thousands. This lowers your initial investment, but there's a big difference in the price you pay for each book. A book self-published with a print run of 1,000 or 2,000 copies might cost you a third as much per copy to produce as you'd pay with a print-on-demand service (the price per book is almost always lower when you print more copies).

	POD Publishing	Self-Publishing	Traditional Publishing
Initial financial investment to create physical books	low	higher	very low
Cost for professional assistance in creating book	moderate	moderate	maybe none
Time to create book	varies	varies	often as long as 12 to 18 months
Ease of making updates	somewhat easy	very easy	difficult
Free help with marketing	no	no	usually
Editorial and design freedom	high	high	moderate to low
Free professional help with jacket and interior design	no	no	yes

Profit margin per book	depends	depends	low compared to POD and self-publishing
Need to do marketing of your own	Yes!	Yes!	Yes!

eCourses

An eCourse offers information delivered to people in increments, electronically. A simple eCourse might consist of a series of four to eight consecutive e-mails on a particular topic, sent at intervals, and it might involve no homework, exercises, or interaction with the instructor. A more complex eCourse might involve dozens of lessons, each delivered sequentially to the purchaser by request when he finishes the previous lesson—or accessed by him on a private, secure Webpage that your customer can't find unless you give her the Web address. An eCourse may involve assignments the customer completes on her own and sends back to you for feedback. It may also involve "class discussion" in a chat room or on a teleseminar, or an audio portion. To find an example of an eCourse, do an online search for "free eCourse" or for "eCourse" and a subject.

One advantage to eCourses that allow for interaction with your customers is that you can learn from your students and glean ideas for future products as you consider their questions and comments. You can also use eCourses to try out new ideas and exercises you're honing and get feedback to help you develop a larger program that you might solidify in a larger eCourse or a book.

Mentoring, Coaching, and Consulting Programs

A mentor (or coach or consultant) is someone who shares her acquired wisdom with others who are less knowledgeable, and offers personalized guidance. You can do one-to-one mentoring or mentoring to a small group. A customer may prefer one-to-one mentoring because he wants privacy (for instance, he might not want others to know about the products he's developing or the specifics of his business), or he feels one-to-one guidance is very valuable to him. Another customer might prefer group mentoring because it offers the advantage of being able to listen to other people discuss issues that will give him information and insights he can apply to his own situation. Then, too, with group mentoring, students can support each other with ideas and encouragement, and may even go on to form a social media networking group after the mentoring program ends so that they can continue to help each other. The potential for students to meet and network with others who share their interests gives your small-group mentoring package value. And as with eCourses, the interaction with your students gives you opportunities to hone your material, create a program based on exercises you've tried out with people, and get ideas for future products.

eCourse, Mentoring: Pros	eCourse, Mentoring: Cons
No need to set up a physical classroom, rent a room, etc.	No physical interaction or real-time interaction with students.
Can try out new ideas if you are interacting with students.	Students may need some technological ability if the course requires interaction and homework.
Potential to get one-to-one clients and, as a result of working with them, get ideas for new products.	

Monthly Subscription Services

A subscription service offers delivery of something of value each month. You can call it a club—for instance, there's The Million Dollar Author Club, and the Book of the Month Club. Your customers are paying for the convenience of having information, or, perhaps, a product, delivered directly to them like clockwork.

The key to a subscription service or club that clients pay to belong to is reliable delivery of valuable information. An example of a profitable subscription is Steve and Bill Harrison's Million Dollar Author Club. Their model is to charge members a small amount for the first month or two and allow them to cancel membership at any time; after that, a monthly fee is automatically charged to the member's credit card. The low introductory fee combined with the valuable information people receive encourages them to decide to try out the service.

Many people find subscriptions, similar to eCourses, a convenient way to receive information. Remember my example of the service that offers books sent to you via e-mail in small, sequential chunks? This is a type of subscription service that appeals to people's need for convenience and having discipline imposed upon them (after all, they could buy the book, carry it around with them, and read it at intervals throughout the day). Think about what your potential customer's busy day is like, and how he might appreciate having products or services delivered to him in this convenient way for a monthly fee.

Then, too, some people prefer one format to another: text, audio, or video. Your subscription-only club may deliver information in any or all of these formats.

Subscription Service: Pros	Subscription Service: Cons
Inexpensive to produce.	Many newsletters are free so it may be challenging to find subscribers who will pay (but not necessarily).
Can be sent irregularly.	
Builds your brand's visibility.	
Can be created and sent quickly.	

Packages Containing Several eProducts and Products

Earlier, I said that you may want to offer your customers more or less information, in one format or another, as part of a large package of information that represents a commitment on their part or as a single product. With information-based products, it's easy to come up with packages that conveniently combine products for your customers.

People have different preferences about formats, so it's advantageous to offer your information in a variety of packages that combine audio, video, and text elements. In fact, someone might like to read a book and later listen to a related audio, and then view a video that demonstrates the ideas presented in the book, then attend a teleseminar or join a small-group mentoring program you host, or hire you to coach them one-to-one. The possibilities for different ways of presenting your material are endless.

Here is a formula for presentation of information that includes many different products you can sell or give away to your clients:

~ Host a teleseminar or Webinar series that provides an opportunity for your clients to make a big commitment to learning about a topic.

~ Include a workbook in the form of an eBook.

~ Include an inspirational audio piece. This could be a meditation or a recording of affirmations that will help your customer build his confidence. Your customers could download the audio file or receive it from you on a CD that you ship to them.

~ Include an audio interview or two that you conducted with experts on specific subtopics or related topics. Again, these could be an audio file or a CD.

~ Include a PowerPoint presentation of the notes. You can include screen shots of Website pages, photographs, line drawings, cartoons, text in the form of short notes and bullet points, and even a video. (However, keep in mind that whenever you're transferring video files electronically, it can take a lot of time. You can also post the video on a public video-sharing site, which students can easily access; that way, you don't use up bandwidth on your site.)

~ Allow your attendees to access a transcription of the entire course, including the question-and-answer session at the end, as a pdf and as a Word document.

~ Include a one-to-one session with each attendee. (If you do this, of course, you'll have to limit the number of attendees based on your availability for one-to-one sessions.)

~ Let your attendees know that there will be time allotted for addressing any of their questions and how they can pose them to you (via e-mails, a Q&A session, and so on).

The possibilities are endless, and the more ways you repackage your information, the greater your potential for reaching customers who prefer to receive information in one form rather than another.

Are you excited about creating your product? Do you have a good sense of what type of product would best serve your customers' needs and work well for you at this time? I hope so. But before we get into the actual production of information-based eProducts, I want you to learn more about three key elements in any successful viral explosion: your passion, prosperity consciousness, and partners.

Chapter 5

Passion!

What's motivating you to launch a viral explosion on the Internet? If the first answer that comes to mind is "money," that's great. There's nothing wrong with wanting to make money. What I'm suggesting is that you consider choosing a more powerful motivator: your personal passion. When it's passion driving you, the revenue and abundance will come naturally, and, sometimes, in some unexpected ways.

My own passion is to make a positive contribution to the lives of others, and the Internet provides a fantastic vehicle for me to do that. As an author, I know how challenging it is to market a book and I understand that deep desire to get the book into the hands of those who will benefit from it the most. Being an entrepreneur, I understand the desire to have a successful, profitable business. And as a former single mother (I was single at the time I started to do this—I'm now happily remarried), I know what it is like to have a passion to provide for my family. Those passions fuel me day to day, keeping me positive in the face of any challenges that arise. I believe passion takes you to greater and greater levels of creativity and enthusiasm.

A while back, a man named Matt Harding, who loved to travel, decided to make a goofy video to amuse himself and his friends, and uploaded it onto the Internet (wherethehellismatt.com). Wherever he went, whether it was Bhutan, the Netherlands, or Zanzibar, he had someone shoot footage of him doing a silly little dance in front of a landmark, beautiful scenery, or a group of people. Sometimes, passersby were amused and joined in, dancing to their own beat. Matt's passion was infectious. He created a video that was entertaining, that touched upon people's own desire to get out and connect with others and find joy. The video also felt fresh and original, and people were excited to be able to pass it along to their friends by simply posting a link to it in an e-mail or on a social networking site, knowing that this simple action would bring a laughter and warmth to their friends who viewed it. Something in that video struck an emotional chord with viewers and it went viral.

Then Matt Harding was contacted by Stride Gum, because they wanted to sponsor him to expand upon his video. They offered to pay his way to travel to more countries and acquire more footage of happy people doing his funny little dance along with him, if he would simply place a title page at the end of the video advertising their product. More than 14 million people have viewed the latest version of the video. Now that's a viral explosion!

Some might say this is the Law of Attraction at work, in which your sheer joy and appreciation for what you have in your life creates a vibration of abundance that attracts to you situations that reflect that abundance. Some might just say that happiness is infectious and if you give to others even in a small way there will be a reward. I see it as an example of how viral explosions can be much larger than you anticipated when you infuse them with passion, and they can generate a lot more revenue and abundance than you would have dreamed (my guess is he wasn't expecting any financial payoff for his pet project, much less the money to travel to 39 countries!). This fellow just loved to visit unusual places and have a laugh dancing in his awkward, funny way. I think his dedication to this adventure shows it was his passion that served as the rocket fuel for success.

By now, you may have an idea of what it is you want to sell. If you're fairly certain it can generate some income for you, that's terrific, but before going forward, be sure that your heart is truly engaged. Going forth with passion is like setting off on a journey with a full gas tank; it will keep you progressing toward your goal.

The process of launching your own viral explosion is going to be rewarding and exciting, and the way to amplify all of those wonderful emotions is to start with enthusiasm, joy, and curiosity. Connect with your passion, let it influence what products you create and how you design your Internet marketing campaign, and keep a steady supply of that rocket fuel flowing your way!

I think if you look beyond your products to their effect on people, you'll be able to put your finger on what really inspires you: the ability to express yourself or share your wisdom or expertise and make a difference in someone's life, even if in a small way.

Passion→Confidence→Creativity→ Success!

Passion comes from a place inside of you where you generate all the positive emotions. These feelings allow you to adopt positive beliefs, blast away any obstacles standing in your way, and take effective, creative action. My fuel is my strong desire to help others achieve their goals and live the life of their dreams, or, as I say on my Website, "Making a positive difference in the lives of millions of others." In fact, my passion is my purpose. But it doesn't matter what your passion is or what you have to offer others—it could be investment advice, information about great wines, or widgets—you must believe wholeheartedly that what you're selling has value. If your business is rooted in personal passion, you're far more likely to achieve success.

When passion is fueling you, it's easier to be flexible, resilient, and creative, all valuable assets when things don't go as planned—and things sometimes don't go as planned. A few years ago, I launched a viral explosion around a CD set called *Magnet for Money,* and realized very late in the process that I needed to special-order what they call clam-shell containers to protect the CDs, which, because they were larger than my original containers, required me to find custom-size boxes. I had no idea where to buy them and was working against an extremely tight deadline.

This unexpected challenge might have thrown me completely off schedule, or cost me a lot of money and jeopardized my profits. However, I chose not to see the situation that way. Because I was connected to my passion and free from fear, I asked myself, "How might I transform this situation into an opportunity to provide even more benefit for my customers? And where should I look to find the solution?"

From experience, I know that the best way to tap into creativity and discover solutions and opportunities is to stay positive and generate feelings of confidence and faith. Rather than immediately starting to think about how I could fix the problem at hand, I started imagining myself packing the boxes and dropping them off at the post office. Then, in my mind's eye, I saw people receiving the packages, opening them up, dropping the first CD into their CD player, and saying aloud, "Wow, this is amazing stuff! I can't believe how great this information is! I'm so glad I found this program. This Peggy McColl really knows what she's talking about."

By spending just a minute or two writing and directing this uplifting visualization, I was able to regenerate confidence in myself and my product, and awaken my ability to think differently. Then I searched the Internet for more information and contacted some people I knew who had sold similar products, and eventually, found a reasonably priced source for the shipping materials I needed. I adjusted my shipping and handling charges to account for my increased expenses.

By connecting to my passion for helping people to achieve their goals, I was able to replace my fear with faith—in myself, in the value of my product, and in my success. I knew that the excitement and joy I felt whenever I imagined helping someone achieve his or her goal would open the pathways to my creativity and the solution would come to me.

In the last chapter of this book, I'll help you plan your launch to make it go as smoothly as possible. Be sure to regularly connect with your true passion so that your journey will be smooth and enjoyable and you'll stay on course, your eyes open to all the opportunities that will present themselves.

Plug Into Your Passion

If passion is your greatest power source, be sure to recharge your batteries and plug into it regularly. One way to do this is to have a mission statement and read it aloud regularly, with great enthusiasm and feeling. Believe in your mission, wholeheartedly.

Another way I reconnect with my passion is by using what I call a Feel Good Bucket in my office. The Feel Good Bucket is simply a bin where I store letters and cards of gratitude and praise I've received from clients and affiliates through the years. I also have a Feel Good Folder stored in my e-mail, where I keep the electronic messages of thanks I've been sent. Whenever I'm having a challenging day, I pull out a handful of papers from my Feel Good Bucket or click on my Feel Good Folder and start reading. I'm reminded of the value of what I'm doing and how much it's appreciated, and that re-energizes me. I believe that if you boost your confidence and remind yourself that you have something of value to offer because you have taken the time to become an expert on the topic of your passion, you'll be able to better serve your customers.

Yet another way to reconnect with your passion is to make time to do what got you excited about your message, product, or area of expertise in the first place. That may seem obvious, but it's very easy to get caught up in the business of business and lose touch with why you're working so hard. Make the time to engage in the activities that fill you with enthusiasm and remind you of why you're spending time on hold waiting for tech support or going over your receipts with your accountant.

Sometimes, the easiest way to connect to your passion is to connect to the people it affects. I love doing teleseminars and writing books, but one of the reasons I travel, make speeches, and do workshops is because I am inspired when I see the faces of people who appreciate the information I'm sharing with them. Get out there and look into your customers' eyes if you can. It will inspire you and remind you why you're working so hard.

How Fear Sabotages Success

Are you eager to make your viral explosion work, or are you "anxious" to make it work? I ask because if you're anxious about making money or a big splash, if you're holding on to fear that you won't be successful, which is going to hamper you and sabotage your success. If you're operating out of fear that you won't have enough money, or that you don't have the expertise to provide value, it doesn't matter how clever or unique your product is because that fear will destroy your confidence and your drive to keep going. Your creative abilities will shut down and you'll be coming from a mindset of scarcity. This often leads to wrong decisions, as Steve, who had attended my seminar on making money on the Internet, discovered.

Steve had promised a new customer that he'd be able to provide a particular service on a tight deadline. He'd had some doubts at first, not about the quality of his service, but about the timing of his project. Steve had always been able to juggle his schedule to accommodate unforeseen circumstances in the past, but this was different. He was short on cash flow and too eager to make a sale. His instincts told him that one of his current projects was likely to take extra time due to circumstances beyond his control. Nevertheless, he was afraid of losing this new customer because his cash flow wasn't very good, and he wanted the security of knowing that he would be able to jump into a new, lucrative project quickly.

Steve agonized over having to tell his customer that he was not going to be able to provide the service he'd sold them on unless their deadline was pushed back. This fear wore away at his faith in himself and sent him into a panic. He chose to remain silent and do everything he could to get the work done, but the result was that he missed the deadline, the client was dissatisfied, and Steve felt terrible about himself. When he began to work with me one-to-one to learn more about how he could market his service on the Internet, I could hear the self-doubt and pessimism in his voice. Finally, after I gently questioned where all this insecurity was coming from, he told me the story. We talked about what had gone wrong and he came to understand that it was his own fear of disappointing his new customer, and not having enough money, that caused him to promise more than he could comfortably deliver.

Together, Steve and I worked on creating some affirmations and visualizations he could use to help him get into the right frame of mind to launch a viral explosion. He reconnected with his passion that was at the core of his business, and regained his confidence that his expertise was so valuable that there would be plenty of customers eager to sign up for his services. A few weeks later, when Steve checked in with me, he happily reported that he'd acquired several new clients, and fearlessly turned down another who wanted him to pay him a lot of money to work on an uncomfortably tight deadline.

Passion gives you that extra enthusiasm for improving on the quality of your product and attending to the important details. You'll become clearer on what you most need to do, whether it's rewrite your sales copy or start contacting potential affiliates. You'll have patience with customers or potential affiliates who may need more time and more information to come to the decision to take you up on your offer, and you'll feel energized throughout the entire process of creating all the elements of a successful viral explosion.

So turn up the volume on your passion and you may find that the sky's the limit, as author Elle Newmark discovered.

A Passion to Be Published: Novelist Elle Newmark

Elle Newmark had a simple dream: to have her novel published. She'd been writing for years, and her novel, *Bones of the Dead*, was a labor of love that she'd carefully crafted and now wanted to find an agent for because she knew that was the first step in selling the book to a publisher. She sent queries to literary agents and got one nibble, so she sent her manuscript in and was thrilled when the agent decided to represent it. The agent submitted it to some publishing houses one by one and kept getting rejections. Elle and the agent parted ways, and she then found a second agent, but the results were the same—no interest from publishers. Elle was frustrated by this slow, traditional process. She was more than 60 years old, and felt time was ticking away because she'd just spent many months getting nowhere closer to achieving her goal. Elle decided to self-publish the book and use the Web to market it, and signed up for my class on how to make your book a best-seller.

Elle was intimidated by Internet marketing at first because of her lack of technical knowledge and familiarity with the World Wide Web. She told me, "I don't know if I can do this, Peggy. I just mastered how to do e-mail!" I told her to get excited and stay connected to her passion because this would give her the patience and courage to push forward and learn all that she needed to know. She took my advice, stayed positive, and felt her creative juices beginning to flow. She decided not to set up a Website or build a subscriber base. Instead, she chose to self-publish her book and sell it to individuals, and at the same time, interest book publishers in purchasing the rights to publish it themselves. She began to focus on producing the book and a landing page that described it.

Once the self-published book had been delivered to her home and the warehouse of an online bookstore, Elle began putting together her virtual book-launch party: She would invite agents and editors to watch what she was doing and see if they wanted to work with her. She knew that novels often get lost in a pile of submissions, and then sent back to her with a form rejection slip. Elle was determined to make her novel stand out, and she would do that by connecting to her passion and reaching out to people on an emotional level. (Remember, if you can establish not just a need but an urgent one—such as an emotional need—you're more likely to achieve success with your product. Elle wanted agents and editors to be just as eager to read her book as she was to find a publisher for it.)

Elle searched the Internet for a list of agents and editors, found a list online, and recorded the agents' e-mail addresses.

Following the advice she'd learned in my course, she decided to offer some bonus gifts for anyone who would buy her novel the day of the launch. Then she set out to handwrite invitations that would go out to her potential affiliates, including those who might have bonus gifts to offer. And then the baking began—yes, baking! Elle got the great idea to bake 1500 bone-shaped cookies to send out to her affiliates, and she packaged them carefully in a box with the handwritten invite to the book launch. In her letter, she reminded them to send out their announcement (with a link to the page of free bonus gifts) to their subscribers on book-launch day. It took her many hours and a lot of flour and eggs, but she soon had her packages ready for the post office.

Elle then created a landing page advertising the book, which featured a link for buying the novel at Amazon.com. A day before she launched her virtual explosion, she sent an e-mail to 400 agents and editors and suggested that they watch the excitement that would unfold the next day! She explained what she'd done and invited them to keep an eye on her sales rankings the following day and contact her with any offers. The day of the launch, her book began selling like crazy, and 10 agents e-mailed her an offer of representation based only on the book's description. And one publisher actually sent her an e-mail with a publishing contract attached!

Elle ended up having two agents compete to sign her up, and she chose one, who worked at a major literary agency. The next week, the book rights went up for auction and a large, established publishing house pre-empted the auction by giving her a 7-figure bid for two books: the novel she'd self-published and another one she'd written. That same day, the book publisher sold the foreign rights to several publishers, generating revenues in the area of the high five figures.

Now, Elle's a very talented writer. If she weren't, she wouldn't have drummed up so much excitement (and revenue!)

after people actually read her self-published novel. However, her story illustrates that passion can push you past obstacles such as stifling rules and a lack of interest from some potential customers. It was her passion that provided the rocket fuel for her viral explosion.

Passion Means Going the Extra Mile

As Wayne Dyer once pointed out, "It's never crowded along the extra mile." Elle could have simply done a mass mailing to her potential clients, and there's nothing wrong with doing a large number of e-mails all at once. But as Elle learned in my class for authors who want to achieve best-sellerdom, a handwritten note is special, and the extra time it takes to write and address each one individually attracts people's attention. If you're going to e-mail people, always use the personal touch.

When you pay attention to the details, you end up with the highest-quality products and campaigns. Passion means you embrace excellence when you create your product or service, and make sure that the buying process is as seamless as possible for your customer. You provide top-notch service that makes a big impression on people. You give them more than they expect. I'll slip an extra CD with valuable information into the package when I send it out to a client who is expecting to receive only the product she paid for. I provide my teleseminar students with even more information and guidance than advertised. I always try to provide the very best service I possibly can, and it's easy to do when I'm operating from enthusiasm and passion.

A Passion for Growth

Another aspect of passion you may not have considered is its potential to grow your business. When you truly love what you're doing, you feel compelled to learn even more than you already know about the trends and technologies. You become interested in related topics and find yourself signing up for classes and workshops that will expand your knowledge base and skills. And, because passion generates positive emotions, it gives you the courage to receive constructive criticism and feedback and use it to hone your products, services, and marketing approaches.

I think it's important to take time now and again to ponder whether there's a way to make your product or presentation even better. It's also a good idea to learn to handle criticism so that you can mine it for its gold. Take the time to let your initial reaction of surprise or disappointment fade, then close your eyes and get in touch with how much you love what you do and how proud you are of what you've created and learned so far. Read some of those letters of praise, congratulations, and thanks from your clients. Then, when you're ready, let yourself become curious about the feedback you received. Is there a way you can improve your product or services? Is there something you can learn? Can you offer even more value to others?

When we reconnect to our passion, and feel good about ourselves and what we have to offer, it's much easier to handle constructive criticism and use it to propel us forward to an even higher level of excellence.

You may find that you only need to make a small change in your product or presentation to solve the problem some people are having. You may come up with an idea for a completely new product or way of serving your customers, or a way of adding value to an existing product or service. That complaint that you contemplated for days may lead you to a valuable insight. Let your passion guide you and strengthen your self-confidence.

Remember, It's YOUR Passion

I've enjoyed many delightful, rewarding partnerships with people throughout the years whose services complemented my product or vice versa. In an ideal world, your passion meets up with another's passion and together you have a baby called success! But not everyone is operating from passion. If you hire people to help you or delegate work, you may be overflowing with passion for your product, service, or message, but the other person may not feel the same way. What's more, he may not feel passionate about his own business. You'll know when someone's in business because she's found her calling and when it's only because she have to pay the mortgage somehow. Pay attention to your instincts about people. If someone seems to lack enthusiasm or is exceptionally negative, or constantly reminds you to keep your expectations of him low, recognize that this is not someone who is operating from passion. You can always attract people who share your strong work ethic, enthusiasm, creativity, and attention to detail. Focus your intention on drawing to yourself the absolute best professional partners, and they will show up. Daily, I say this affirmation with enthusiasm and emotion: "I *only* attract loving, peaceful, kind, appreciative, and honest people into my life and into my business," and you might want to do so as well.

But even though you may well find someone whose passion for her own service or product matches the strength of your own, no one will be as excited about your idea as you are. Team with people, but always remember that this project is your baby, not theirs. Aunties and uncles are great, but you're the parent. Always keep your eye on the big picture and the schedule, and double-check the details when it comes to any task you turn over to others to complete.

Know whom you're hiring and ask questions about exactly what they can do for you. A client of mine, Phil, hired someone to help him market his teleseminar. He wasn't charging for the event but wanted it recorded so that he could sell it later as a download or CD product. The PR marketing firm offered to have one of its people act as the interviewer, and Phil provided questions. However, he didn't ask who this person was and whether this fellow had any experience interviewing. The tele-seminar didn't go well, as the interviewer went off topic and didn't pay attention to the time, so they ended up not covering all the material that had been promised. Phil received some annoyed and angry calls and e-mails from people who had attended and felt they'd been misled. He hoped that at least he could salvage enough material to create a short informational product, but then discovered that the call had not recorded properly and it couldn't be used. He stopped payment to the marketing firm, but the damage was done, and he apologized to his clients and sent them a free e-product to make amends and show them that he was committed to providing value.

Whenever you come from passion, it's easier to recognize when you need help and determine whether someone you'd like to hire truly has the skills and knowledge needed to do the job. Maybe you have such difficulty writing that you truly can't create great sales copy for your Website or landing page, for instance, or maybe you have difficulty doing math and need someone to help you check your figures. Passion helps you to acknowledge any gut instincts that tell you this is not the right partner for you, and it gives you the confidence to keep looking for partners whose passion can match your own. Let's look at that formula again:

Passion → Confidence → Creativity → Success!

A few times, I've had clients call me about my services and I could tell from the tone of their voices and the type of ques-tions they asked that they were too distrustful for me to work with comfortably (usually, they were focused on my fees and guarantees and not much else). Because I'm connected to my passion, I feel confident turning down the offer to work with such clients. I always know that wonderful opportunities and passionate, positive, enthusiastic clients are everywhere, and I can attract them to my business.

When You Need to Switch Direction

If you're truly operating from passion, you will know when you should persist in following the course you're on and when you should switch direction. Passion gives us clarity and the ability to be honest with ourselves. It's important to pay attention if your inner voice says, "I think I could come up with a more effective marketing tool," "It seems I should change tactics if I'm going to convince this person to do me a favor and give me a discount," or "I want to connect with this person and listen more carefully so I can hear what he really needs from me." It allows you to ask questions such as,

~ What can I do even better?

~ How can I be of even more service to my clients?

~ How can I deliver my message in a way that helps people instantly recognize the potential for amazing results?

The confidence that comes from passion will increase your ability to get around obstacles and achieve success, but another important element in a viral explosion is having what I like to call *prosperity consciousness*, which you'll learn about in the next chapter.

Chapter 6

Prosperity Consciousness

Do you have a strong belief that you are worthy of achieving the abundance you desire? Do you feel you offer value to others? A few times, potential customers have said to me, "You should give me your products for free. After all, you already have a lot of money—you don't need any more." I know my products have value and I feel very comfortable when there is an exchange of value and a customer gives me money in exchange for my product. I feel that everyone deserves to be compensated for the value they bring to others. If someone doesn't feel that way, it may be because they have emotional issues surrounding money.

If you want to launch a successful viral explosion, allow yourself to truly believe "I deserve to make money" and "What I have to offer is of great value, so people will be eager to purchase my products." *Prosperity consciousness is the awareness that all of us have something of value to offer, and we all deserve to get paid for what we provide to others.*

One way you may choose to provide value to others is through offering free eProducts that generate traffic to your Website, resulting in an expansion of your subscriber base. Marcia Wieder, who bills herself as America's Dream Coach, wrote 10 free eBooks and found partners willing to promote them to their subscribers as part of a viral explosion. These new subscribers visited her Website, got to know her brand, downloaded her eBooks, and 50,000 of them signed up for her newsletter. Later, as a result of building up her subscriber base, she was able to sell products she created as well as others' products she knew would be of value to her followers and fans.

Although it takes time (and sometimes a small amount of money) to create free eProducts and marketing campaigns, it's a wonderful long-term investment in your business. By maintaining prosperity consciousness—your belief that you have something of value to offer others and you will be compensated for it—you will be better able to figure out if there's room for improvement in your marketing campaigns, or whether you might make your product even better and more valuable.

I always like to say that if you're not in business to do business, you won't be in business for long. Revenue has to come in eventually, but sometimes, people let their prosperity consciousness give way to a fear consciousness that actually makes it more difficult to generate profits. Anxiously, they ask, "How much money can I make, fast?" instead of confidently pondering, "How can I use my skills, talents, and brand to build a self-sustaining business that generates income for me over the long run, a business with profits that continually increase, so that my investment of time and capital can be gradually reduced? And how can I do this while providing something of great value to others?" I have nothing against making money fast, but the fear consciousness that creates that intention of "give me money quick!" without any thought to the health of your business in the long-run, rarely seems to lead to big profits, brand-building, or business growth. It's a mentality that leads to cutting corners, offering inferior products, overpricing products that have value but not as much as their price would indicate, and creating ill-will among customers who feel they haven't gotten their money's worth. It's prosperity consciousness that leads to quality products, thinking things through, proper pricing, and highly effective Internet marketing campaigns.

When you approach your business decisions with confidence and faith, you make good choices, and profits result. So adopt prosperity consciousness and repeat after me:

*I deliver great value to others and I am
richly rewarded for it.*

I am worthy of payment for my exceptional services.

*My customers are happy to pay me, and they are
thrilled with the exceptional value they receive and
they keep coming back for more.*

Now you are ready to figure out what your products and services are worth in the marketplace!

What Is Your Time Worth?

One of the biggest mistakes you can make is to underestimate what your time is worth. Time is money, so use it wisely or you're going to be working a lot of hours for very little payback. (Even if your bottom line isn't profit but outreach, it makes sense to use your time efficiently so that your message gets out to the largest number of people).

As you begin the process of figuring out the prices of your products, think about what your time is worth. Let's say you're starting out and have to invest many hours in preparation of your teleseminar, and you end up with 10 attendees.

Now you're making $1,000 to host it, but when you divide that amount by the time spent preparing it (let's say six hours) and hosting it (four hours), you're making $100 an hour to give the presentation. If you're charging $200 an hour for personal mentoring, that may not seem like a good investment of your time. However, your teleseminar attendees who haven't worked with you before may be so impressed by the information they receive in those four hours that several of them decide to hire you at $200 an hour for one-to-one coaching, and then they tell their friends about you. Because you've created the course already, you can run it again and again and register even more people for the class. In addition, because you'll be recording the teleseminar, you'll now have an audio product you can sell or reshape into an eBook and sell (or, later on, give away to build your business). As you can see, this type of offering can escalate into much bigger opportunities.

You can choose to work with individuals and with larger groups. You might find it very emotionally rewarding to mentor people. And if you're just starting out and getting a feel for how to present your material in a way that's most beneficial for others, you may want the comfort and confidence that comes with working with a small number of people at one time. You can get their immediate feedback, which will help you further hone your material and presentation so you can provide even more value in the future.

Consider Whether to Hire Others to Help You

As you sketch out a budget for your viral explosion, and plan your time, think about whether you want to hire people to take over some of the work for you. If you're short on time, or you don't have the skills needed for a particular task, you can hire someone to help you. If I'm able to teach a teleseminar that's going to generate $10,000 in revenue in four hours, I don't want to take 10 hours, unpaid, to work on editing videos when I can find someone to do that for far less than $2,500 an hour. Also, I don't particularly enjoy video editing, and I haven't learned how to do it well so I'm not very efficient at it. It's better for me to focus on the purpose of creating those videos and how I'm going to use them than to take the time to learn video editing.

Michael Gerber, author of *The E-Myth,* has pointed out that to be a successful entrepreneur you have to wear three hats. First, you have to be the technician who makes sure the job gets done right whether you're the teacher, the coach, or the advisor. Second, you have to be the manager who organizes tasks and stays on top of the budget. Third, you have to be the entrepreneur who has a larger vision of what the business can be. He says you have to work *on* your business more than *in* your business: If you've always got your head down as you focus completely on the everyday activities that you need to be involved in as the technician, you may find you're working too hard because you aren't taking on the tasks of a manager or an entrepreneur. If you have difficulty with organization and accounting and finances, improve on these skills and consider hiring professionals to help you. And to step in to your entre-preneurial role, make sure you schedule time for pondering the big picture. Research what others are doing, brainstorm with other creative people, and keep imagining new ways of doing business.

If you don't have much money to invest in your business or in a viral explosion, then you may want to spend the time doing many of the jobs yourself as best you can until you can afford to hire someone. Consider, too, the possibility of free labor. Students and people just beginning their businesses may be willing to do work for you in exchange for a testimo-nial for their own work. You might also swap work, getting free Website design in exchange for writing promotional copy for your Web designer. Your friends and family might be willing to pitch in for free, whether it's a niece who can help you learn how to use shopping-cart software or your husband who can help you stick address labels on mailing envelopes. And sometimes, people you know will be willing to give you a discount on their services or free advice simply because you asked, because they remember how difficult it was when they were first starting out. If you can't afford to pay them, thank them profusely and promise to "pay it forward" and help someone else later on, and return the favor someday if you can.

Build Your Presence, Create Good Will

Profits matter, but it's what we can contribute to the world and what we can bring to our relationships with our clients, subcontractors, suppliers, and peers that's most important. It's understandable that we all want to build strong connections to others even as we're developing our business's reputation. We interact with others in the course of everyday business, but we also need to do outreach in other ways, from lectures and workshops to media appearances, radio interviews, articles, and interaction on social media sites. However, all of this outreach should fit into your overall business plan.

It's very easy to get caught up in social networking in particular, and not have a clear sense of whether it's ultimately helping you generate revenue. Some people believe you should follow a specific formula such as "do 30 posts a day on social networking sights to keep your customers interested in your brand because that's the only way to be heard above the noise." That formula may be true for some business owners, but does it work for *you*?

Think about the people whose posts you want to read— not just people who have a similar business to yours, but people who seem to be creating loyal followers. Notice what they're posting, and how often they're posting. If they rarely post, or seem to bombard you with nuggets of information or observations that don't have much value to you, you probably aren't engaged by their posts. My guess is that there's at least one entrepreneur in your social network whose comments are so entertaining, engaging, insightful, provocative, or helpful that you find yourself regularly reading them. Take a cue from people like this as you decide what to post, and determine what works for you.

Blogging is another example of a marketing strategy that can take up a lot of hours with little payoff if you're not careful. Ask yourself, "Do I really need to blog daily or more than once daily, constantly providing information? Is that time that would better spent dreaming up new products or planning a viral explosion?" What are you accomplishing with your blog? Are you building a community or just wracking your brain for hours each week trying to write a 400-word post? For many people, that much writing can feel overwhelming. I've seen effective, engaging blog posts that are very short, that perhaps comment on an article for which the blogger provides a link. You can use a Web camera to do a video blog post, too. Look at blogs you enjoy and try to determine what it is about them that works about their way of communicating, and you'll get some ideas on how you might blog effectively.

If you suspect you're spending too much time on these marketing techniques, actually log how much time you spend on these activities in a typical week. Then ask yourself, what would the results be if you spent that much time in activities that might have a greater payoff? You may want to use a kitchen timer or software that flashes a "time's up!" message after you've spent a certain amount of time on social media sites. And you may want to set a goal for blogging less often but promoting that blog better, and collecting your blog pieces into a book.

What Is Your Product Worth?

At this moment in time, it's easier to figure out the price of tangible objects such as a CD set or a book than it is to determine what to charge for an information-based product in a less established medium. If you go to a bookstore, you'll quickly be able to determine the range of prices for a typical hardcover or softcover book. But if you created an eBook that's approximately the same length as a standard book, would people be willing to pay the same amount, or even more?

What makes pricing so tricky is that even if you can find examples of similar products (and I encourage you to do your research), you have to evaluate whether or not your product is of greater or lesser value than those other products. That's why when I'm coming up with prices, I will often simply ask myself, "What would I pay for this?" or "What would someone else, who is looking for this type of product, pay for this?"

I've seen eBooks sell for a few dollars and a few hundred dollars—one book promised all the secrets to getting yourself booked on a hugely popular talk show, a show with a proven ability to sell books written by its guests. Clearly, that book had great value for authors wanting to appear on that particular talk show, especially because the only other way to attain that information was to somehow get access to a producer for the show and speak to her. You may also want to think about whether your product or service will help people earn money or save money, which would justify assigning it a higher price tag.

Remember, people will pay for convenience. Is yours the only product featuring valuable information in a video form for people who prefer to learn by watching a video than reading a book? Does your book contain more guidance and ideas than any other book on the topic?

Finally, think about your brand and the value you offer. Very few people out there are delivering high-quality products and services and running their business with total integrity, genuineness, and heart, with the intent of not just making money but serving others. Don't underprice your products and services out of a false fear that there's too much competition out there and you have to undercut your rivals. Your rivals may not be providing high quality and service.

> **Tip**
>
> If you offer your customer a guarantee, it may give him that extra reassurance he needs to commit to buying your product. Guarantees provide great value. I offer a $95 CD set, and on the package I state my promise that if you purchase it and apply my advice, and feel you didn't get more than your money's worth, and you contact me within 30 days of purchase, I'll refund your money (excluding shipping and handling) as long as you return the CDs in excellent condition. A money-back guarantee may actually double your sales.

Three Types of Prices: High, Low, and Free

The first product or service you create and launch a viral explosion around can be priced low or high. I don't think it matters which as long as the price reflects the value (you can also make a free product the focus of your viral explosion, and you'll learn more about why you might want to do that shortly). As you build your business, you should consider offering products in three price ranges: high, low, and free.

A big-ticket item or high-priced service represents a commitment of money and emotion. If your customer wants to start up a business for the first time, improve her communication with her spouse or her teenage daughter, prevent a disease that runs in her family, or learn a skill she knows will allow her to make much more money than she's currently earning, she may be willing to pay a few hundred or even a few thousand dollars for information that will help her with those goals that are dear to her heart. How many people start out the new year by signing up for an expensive diet program, or invest in a high-end piece of exercise equipment, by way of telling themselves that truly, this is the year they're going to lose weight and get healthier? A big investment represents a big emotional commitment that people want to make to improve their lives in some way, or solve a problem that's been bothering them.

A lower-priced (or moderately priced) item may represent a bargain to people. If you can offer great value in a $10 to $50 product, even people who might not have a strong emotional commitment might say, "I'll try it. What do I have to lose? A few dollars." When they discover that they've gotten more than their $20 worth, they will feel they've found a tremendous bargain and will appreciate that you offered them this marvelous value. They're likely to tell their friends about your product and you, and subscribe to your newsletter to learn more about what you have to offer. One day, when you announce a $300 product or even a $2,000 product, they may well say, "That, too, is probably a huge bargain given how much this person delivered on that $20 product I bought." You will have built your reputation as someone who offers value.

That brings us to free products. There's a misconception that to gain customers you must offer all your information for free and hope that your Website's click ads will generate enough revenue to make up for what you're giving away. For some sites, this works, but for many, it's not a profitable model. Often, what works best is to give away free *samples* of your services or materials, or to give away one or more free bonus gifts, which will build good will and may inspire your customers to buy something from you later. Just as with a lower-priced product, a free product generates lots of interest from customers who want a bargain, and builds your reputation and subscriber list.

If you're doing a viral explosion and have no Website or subscriber base, create at least one bonus gift if not two or three. If you have a Website, put up some free information or offer a free eCourse. In fact, it's important that if you do have a site, you offer some free content, not just advertising for your products.

One of the concerns I've heard from people is, "What if I put all my secrets in my book? Then they won't come to my teleseminars or hire me to be a consultant or coach." If you have a *scarcity mindset* rather than *prosperity consciousness*, you'll buy into the myth that you have to hoard the knowledge you have rather than sharing any of it for free. You'll be afraid to put too much information into a product that people will purchase and use because you'll mistakenly believe it will fill all their needs and they'll never come back. Actually, what usually happens is if you do offer value, people want *more*—more personalized service, more information on a related topic, more interaction with you, more encouragement and hand-holding, and so on. Be generous and provide value at a good price. And then get ready to upsell and suggestive sell.

The Power of Upselling and Suggestive Selling

Suggestive selling and upselling meet your clients' need for *more*. People can be very brand loyal. Once your customers are sold on your brand, they will keep coming back to see what else you have to offer.

With upselling, you provide something of great value at a reasonable or low cost, or even free, and then offer another fantastic, higher-priced product that you believe your customer would also enjoy. Suggestive selling is similar, but instead of offering a higher-priced product, you're offering a valuable product for a similar or lower price. Retail stores and restaurants use these techniques when they offer a price-fixed dinner and then, after you've ordered that discounted meal, the waiter suggests a bottle of wine (with a high markup) with your dinner. Because you got a bargain on the chicken marsala, you figure, heck, why not splurge and have a little wine, too? In teleseminars, it's common for the host to focus on giving the rock-solid advice the customers paid to receive, and then mention here and there that if the listeners stick around to the end of the call, they can learn details about an amazing product that will meet their need for more information and more guidance.

People will respond to upselling because you've won their trust by proving you have value to offer them, and you're even willing to give some of it to them for free or a low price. But when you upsell, keep in mind your audience; don't assume they would be interested in anything you have to sell. If people are attending your teleseminar on how to improve their cooking skills, don't try to upsell them a fantastic product you created that will teach them how to improve their golf swing. The products you offer have to be similar in some way to the product you're upselling from.

Another way to upsell or suggestive sell is through your shopping-cart function or Website. Some of the more popular sites for buying domain names and hosting services automatically add all sorts of services you might want, and you'll have to click on the check boxes to take them out of your cart (it's sort of like a little kid at the grocery store dropping bags of cookies and candy into your cart when you're not looking!). I don't suggest you necessarily choose such an aggressive upselling or suggestive-selling program to be embedded into your software, but by all means, if someone's buying your book, he should see an ad for your CD-set or your previous book before he checks out. When someone's in a buying mood with her credit card out, it's the perfect time to approach her to buy something else. You might also add value by giving away a free item at checkout, or dropping a free bonus gift into the box before you ship a product to your customer. If people associate your brand with value and see that you're willing to give them something for free, will feel good about spending more money than they intended and trying a new product they're not totally certain about.

As you consider how to price your products, keep in mind the value of what you're offering and the credibility of your brand. Then, once you've set aside any disempowering beliefs that might hold you back, you'll need to learn about one of the most important elements of a viral explosion, a key to Internet marketing that holds tremendous potential for unlocking success for you: Partners.

Chapter 7

Partners

No matter how strong your brand or how valuable your product you can't achieve success all on your own. You need partners to help you. It's great to spread the word through family and friends and a small number of loyal customers, but to get your message out there in a big way, you have to reach a mass audience. So, to create a viral explosion, you'll need *affiliates*. Affiliates are owners of e-mail lists who are willing to help you reach a larger audience with your message, and willing to offer your product to their customers. Usually, but not always, affiliates receive a percentage of the revenue you receive for any sales made to their followers (note that this type of *affiliate marketing* can also be applied to viral explosions based on free products—obviously, in this case, there's no revenue from sales).

Getting the word out about your brand is vital for the growth of your business, and offering free products, bonus gifts, discounts, and limited-time offers is a great way to grab people's attention and excite them about what you have to offer, whether it's a specific product, guidance, a service, entertainment, an uplifting message, or something else.

When you have prosperity consciousness, it's easier to be confident that you will find affiliates by contacting people you don't know, even people who are quite successful and whom you might feel intimidated approaching. If you truly have something of great value to offer their subscribers, they'll most likely be willing to listen to you. The effort you're asking them to make is minimal, and everyone benefits: you, them, and their subscribers. They need only to send out an e-mail to their list on a particular day, with copy you created that explains the benefits and value of your product. In that e-mail, they'll include an affiliate link you've provided, which their subscriber can use to access your landing page and shopping cart. Technology does the rest.

Even so, many entrepreneurs can be reluctant to make those cold calls to potential partners, because they don't want to hear "No, I'm not interested." Remember, they're not rejecting you, they're rejecting a business opportunity. And they may be saying no simply because they need more information to convince them to participate in your viral explosion. If you're prepared, you may well be able to give them enough information to get past their initial reluctance, as you'll see.

Important Points About Affiliate Marketing

~ You do *not* have to have your own database list to do affiliate marketing.

~ I do *not* recommend that you buy any lists, which results in creating spam.

~ There are millions of Websites on the Internet today, so the number of potential affiliates for you is huge.

It is possible that you'll encounter people who don't recognize the potential in participating in your Internet marketing campaign. They may not realize that people have made millions of dollars with this business strategy, and even those with a shoestring budget have been able to achieve success and provide value using this formula. It's time-consuming to find affiliates, to be sure, but if you can find owners whose lists are a good match for your product, you'll do well. And remember, once you've set up affiliate relationships with others, you can help them and they can help you, and everyone's customers or followers benefit.

Why Affiliate Marketing Is So Effective

A viral explosion happens when one person's passion energizes others. Because we're more likely to trust the word of people we know, positive word-of-mouth advertising is extremely effective. Offline, the difficulty with relying on this form of promotion is that people are busy and aren't always able to get together in person, and when they do, they may not find themselves in a conversation in which they happen to mention how terrific your product is. Online, however, it's a completely different picture. Post to a social networking site, and hundreds or thousands of people may be reading what you have to say. If you have a few hundred followers, and a good number of them respond to your post by reposting what you've said, or writing up their own post recommending your services, in a matter of minutes you can reach thousands of people via personal recommendations.

Is this really the same as one-to-one, word-of-mouth endorsements? I believe it is similar, only much faster and far more effective. If you felt that a friend or acquaintance of yours on a social media site was simply promoting products he didn't believe in for the purpose of making money, you'd pick up on that and realize you couldn't trust his recommendations. Similarly, if someone at work kept promoting her brother's auto body shop, you might take her at her word, but then, if you took your car to his shop and he did a poor job, it could affect your relationship with her. The incentive to be honest with the people you know and care about is very high.

In fact, when you approach your potential affiliates about participating in a viral explosion, it's a good idea to ask them if, in addition to sending an e-mail to their subscribers, they'd be willing to post about your offer on social media sites they use. It's a wise strategy. Not everyone will regularly check particular social networking sites. And besides, subscribers may be receiving the e-mailed newsletter but not be reading it these days. You're more likely to gain their attention if your affiliate sends out your message using more than one medium. (The FTC has regulations about promoting products and services for profit on social networking sites, Websites, and blogs. These are posted at *www.ftc.gov*, and you should review them in order to be sure that your Internet marketing campaign is in alignment with their rules.)

Why Someone Would Want to Be Your Affiliate and Promote Your Product

There are several reasons a list owner may be willing to promote your products. First, he or she may simply want to help. You might be surprised by how often complete strangers are willing to give you assistance if you simply ask and they feel your passion for your product, service, or message. Also, affiliates want to offer value to their subscribers, and if they feel your product has value, they'll be willing to participate in your viral explosion to get the word out to their people. And if what you're offering is a valuable product that would generate revenue for him, a list owner has the added incentive of possibly making some money. If the list owner you approach has never participated in a viral explosion, you'll need to explain how the program works as well as pitch your product to her so that she sees its value for her clients and customers. It's helpful if you explain to him that the campaign will create exposure for her. Affiliates usually are featured in a short profile on the landing page for the offer, and if they are also offering a downloadable bonus gift for buyers of your product, they'll typically have a short description of their brand or themselves next to the description of their bonus gift. In addition, because people will be visiting their Website as a result of their offering bonus gifts as part of your campaign, they have an opportunity to build their e-mail list.

Sometimes, a list owner won't need much of a pitch from you because she believes so strongly in your brand that she trusts that what you're offering will be of interest to the people on her list. She may be a friend or long-time associate who wants to help you out, even if there's no financial profit in it for her.

Also, even if the product you're offering is free, you can set it up so that the affiliate might earn some revenue. Using your shopping-cart software, you can offer your affiliates an ID or code number. If their follower clicks through that link to reach your site to download a bonus gift, and then the follower chooses to buy a product from you later on, as long as he doesn't clear his computer's "cookies," the shopping cart software will register a commission for the affiliate who originally sent him your way.

The time you've invested in building your brand will help you when you start approaching people to partner with you. Think about any groups you've been involved with, even if just online as a subscriber, that might be able to partner with you. Your product or services may appeal strongly to members of community organizations, women's networks, sales networks, and even support groups. Remember, more than 1.7 billion people are on the Web!

List owners are motivated to provide their customers with value. If they judge that your product, service, or message will benefit their subscribers, and they'll make revenue simply by sending out an e-mail recommendation, it's very likely that they'll want to become your affiliate.

How to Find Potential Affiliates

I subscribed to a number of newsletters on topics related to self-growth, so when I was ready to launch a viral explosion for a self-growth product I'd created, I started looking for affiliates among owners of newsletters with themes of self-growth, holistic health, personal empowerment, and so on.

You can also think about Websites you've visited that might have a newsletter attached to them. *I can't emphasize enough that you don't have to limit yourself to your specific topic.* If you're selling a teleseminar on creating jewelry made from recycled materials, or even if you're selling the jewelry itself, don't simply type into a search engine "jewelry recycled materials" and see what Websites come up. Start there, but also think of sites that sell refurbished clothing, or that appeal to environmentally conscious consumers. You may have more luck partnering with list owners whose interests are very close to yours, but you may also have luck with a site where the subscribers are people interested in fashion—or just women in general!

Once again, let's look at offline marketing as an example of effective techniques. A bakery may team up with a bridal store so that if you buy a wedding gown or accessories, you'll receive a coupon for a discount on a wedding cake from the baker. Meanwhile, the bridal store offers a deal such that if you bring in your receipt for ordering a wedding cake, you can get a discount from the bridal store. On the other hand, bakeries don't just sell wedding cakes (although that is probably their highest-ticket item). They may want to partner with a catering service, an events planner, or a whole foods co-op (if they sell healthy wholegrain cookies, for instance).

So as you consider potential affiliates, "go wide." See the bigger picture. Look for affiliates among your current business associates and among the people you meet at conferences and personal appearances. Look for affiliates using the Internet, too.

Think about what products and services you purchase because of your interests and lifestyle, and what your potential customers are buying right now. What other Websites do you visit? What sites might they visit? Where are your potential affiliates online and offline?

To use the Internet to find potential affiliates, search online for specific keywords related to your topic, and look at what click ads and Websites come up. Sign up for newsletters and eCourses from sites you're interested to get a better feel for how they communicate to their subscribers and who those subscribers might be. If a site does not have an e-mail signup, either on its front page or its contact page, it may not have a subscriber list. However, the site may have a customer e-mail list.

You can also search for a keyword term and "newsletter" or "ezine" to find lists. Then subscribe and familiarize yourself with the style and format of the newsletter. Get a feel for who the subscribers are. Then contact the list owner to see if you can sign him up to become your affiliate.

I also suggest looking for lists of the top Websites on your topic or a topic related to yours, which you can do through a simple search for, say, "top dieting Websites" or "top 10 self-growth Websites." You can consult Websites that rank Website traffic to get a feel for how many people are visiting any particular site.

If you're unsure of the size of a particular list, feel free to ask the owner to reveal it to you if you want to get a sense of how big your outreach is. Reassure him that you're asking simply to get a feel for how many people you'll be reaching in your campaign and that you're happy to work with him regardless of the size of his list (some people are insecure about the modest number of subscribers they have).

Whenever I've done viral explosions, however, I've been more focused on getting partners than on counting up the number of people who will receive an e-mail as part of my campaign. Any particular individual might subscribe to several of the lists, so you really don't know how many unique individuals will be receiving an e-mail about your offer. Also, some lists may be very large yet will yield few responses to your product, whereas a very small list might yield many responses. But you may find it reassuring to know how many people are receiving notice of your offer. For my first viral explosion, I needed to sell my books quickly because of my very large financial investment in those books, so I used just 12 partners, one of whom had a particularly big list and was even willing to forego his affiliate payment. Each was a high-quality list for my type of product. You just never know which lists will yield great results.

Once you've done the research to find affiliates for a viral explosion, you can go back to those affiliates for another viral explosion. What's more, they may come back to you to offer something of value to your own e-mail subscriber list. That's why the time invested in procuring affiliates and building your own list is time well spent. Always be looking for people who might partner with you in the future.

Keep Track of Your Affiliates

Clearly, affiliate marketing requires you to keep track of a lot of information, so from the beginning, keep careful records of the sites you find, the lists and list owners, and your contact with them. I like to do this on an Excel spreadsheet, but you could do it using a different type of software or even a notebook. You'll be very glad you kept such meticulous notes when you go to do an Internet marketing campaign, as well as later, when you are researching potential affiliates again and wondering, "Did I contact this site before?" I like to use two different pages on Excel, one for my initial outreach to list owners, and one for the people who agree to be affiliates.

Some of the categories you should have on your spreadsheet or in your notes are:

~ Website address.

~ Keyword searched to get there.

~ Contact name for Website, e-mail address, city and state, phone number.

~ Does this site owner have a newsletter?

~ Does this site owner take articles?

~ Does this site owner they do giveaways?

~ Your comments and observations.

~ Contacted when?

~ Followed up?

~ Response.

~ On board—how?

The second page, for confirmed affiliates, would typically have the following columns:

~ Sent e-mail copy for them to use with their subscribers.

~ Received confirmation that they'll send the e-mail on launch day.

~ Percentage of sale (if any) they'll receive as commission (because it may vary from affiliate to affiliate).

~ Date commission was paid (this is actually tracked by your shopping-cart software but it's good to have this second record so no one is accidentally overlooked).

How to Approach a Potential Affiliate

Before you actually contact potential affiliates, it's important to be prepared with materials that describe your brand and the benefits of your product, evidence of your credibility, and the product itself. Always double check to make sure your pitch makes it clear to them "what's in it for me." If you can, have your landing page (also known as a sales page, which you'll learn to design and write in Chapter 9) ready. Once you've done a few viral explosions and are familiar with how to write landing pages, and have a good sense of how much time it will take you to set one up, you may wish to focus on signing up affiliates before turning your attention to the creation of the landing page. However, if you've never written a landing page before, you may want do it before making your pitch. You'll have plenty of time to learn how to create effective landing page copy, and then can show list owners the completed landing page, which will provide them with more information about your product.

As for the actual product, you need to have it ready to be delivered so that your potential partner can read it, listen to it, or view it before she commits to promoting it to her list. Even when I've worked with authors whose books weren't published yet, they were able to send potential affiliates a .jpg of the jacket and a file containing the manuscript in lieu of the actual book. (Check with the Federal Trade Commission if you have any concerns about how ready your product must be before you start selling it, as they've changed some rules to stop the most outrageous or unscrupulous sellers.)

The first step in approaching a list owner you'd like to sign up as an affiliate is to check out his Website, sign up for his newsletter, and get a feel for what his message is and who his subscribers are. Then, check his Website's contact page to see how he prefers to be contacted, by phone or e-mail. If his number is listed, go ahead and call him during standard business hours, Monday through Friday, between 9 a.m. and 5 p.m. *his* time (check the time zone). If no one answers, you can leave a message, but don't persist in calling. Instead, if you don't hear back, approach the list owner a second time by e-mail.

Start the conversation by asking if this is a good time to talk. Let him know who you are, express what you know and like about his site and newsletter, then explain that you have a business opportunity that will benefit him and his subscribers, cost him no money, and take only a few minutes of his time. (And if you pitch to him by e-mail, address the list owner personally, by his first name.) In your pitch, offer your potential partner some information about what he'd be selling or offering to his subscribers.

Here's a sample benefit-oriented pitch that could be used on the phone:

Hi Becky! I've been looking at your site, newsletter, and products, and I see that you're very passionate about your work, and you're sharing very high-quality information with parents and teachers. I'm a teacher, too, teaching first and second grade for 18 years. I'd like to help you create even more value for your subscribers, and give you the chance to offer them something they will love and benefit from. It's a $10 eBook I wrote on easy ways to help kids stay focused in the classroom. So many kids have such a hard time of it, and my tips are practical and no cost or low cost, and if you can send an e-mail to your subscribers promoting my book, it won't cost you a penny and it could generate some healthy commissions for you. I would love to get your commitment to participating in my Internet campaign, which will launch on April 21. Can I give you some more details on the program and how it can benefit you and your subscribers and help both of us to make a positive difference in the lives of children?

And if what you're offering in your promotion is a free product, of course, you wouldn't mention commissions as one of the benefits. Then, too, if you've sold the product before, you might want to note some of the results other affiliates have achieved. For instance, I'll say that I cut a check for $1,330 to another affiliate the last time I sold the product.

In your pitch, be concise and get the core points across immediately. You'll also need to tell the list owner what percentage of revenue you'd like to pay him. Then, ask him if he can commit to sending the e-mail to his followers on a particular date. If he has any objections at that point, he can bring them up.

Keep in mind that your approach has to be in synch with your style or brand and theirs. Here are two very different e-mails you could send to potential affiliates to encourage them to learn more about your offering. The first was one I sent to someone I knew very well, and who was (and is) quite familiar with affiliate marketing, so I didn't have to explain the process.

Affiliate e-mail sample #1

Subject: Biggest response ever to this one!

Dear (use the affiliate's first name),

Want something that really "pulls well" and converts to sales? I haven't offered this to any other affiliates yet, I thought I'd start with you.

It's "hot" and people LOVE it because it is for anyone. It's called _____ and it's a program designed to _____. You can see my sales copy here:

http://www.linkgoeshere.com

I'm selling it for $99 (VERY VERY VERY reasonable and I believe that's why so many people respond so well to it). I'll do a 60(me)/40(you) split with you, and I can get you the copy in the next 10 minutes if you want. Please let me know when we can schedule a mailing. Oh yes, the best part, it is a DOWNLOADABLE product—easy to deliver.

Notice the enthusiastic copy and focus on making money.

This next example is for a free eProduct. Again, it's short, sweet, to the point, and directed to the list owner by name.

Affiliate e-mail sample #2

Subject: I Have Something Valuable for Your Clients that Won't Cost Them a Penny!

Dear James,

Are your newsletter subscribers eager for some quick advice on how to save money entertaining this holiday season? I've run a highly successful events-planning business in Chicago for 16 years, putting together every last detail for parties hosted by major companies, socialites, and local celebrities, and made a tidy profit because I know how to do elegance on a shoestring. That's why I've written a 22-page eBook called *Elegant and Economic Entertaining: Tips That Will Make Your Party a Smash Without Breaking Your Piggy Bank*, which I am offering FREE. I feel certain this guide will be of tremendous value to your subscribers this holiday season, so I hope you would be willing to learn some more details at my site (fill in the URL for the landing page), and send a simple e-mail to your subscribers on November 21 with a link to the download.

Please do get back to me by the end of the week with your confirmation to be on board with the November 21 e-mailing!

All the best,

Jane Smith

(your Website address)

If you're really keen on getting a particular list owner to become your affiliate, and you're not getting a response, you might try again after you've signed up other list owners, particularly if one has a name that might impress her or if you have signed up some owners of similar lists. Send an e-mail asking whether this person you're pursuing has had a chance yet to review your materials regarding your product, and mention that you've now partnered with this other big-name person who saw that it was a terrific opportunity, or signed up more than 25 partners (and list a few). Quite often, I've found that people will sign up to be affiliates after they've seen who else chose to participate.

Finally, when you do get a partner to sign on, as you close the deal, thank her, remind her of when you'll be contacting her again and sending her the affiliate link (and, if you're writing it, the copy for her letter to subscribers). Then ask her if she can recommend any other people who might want to become your affiliate.

Should you sense that a list owner is reluctant to participate, try to figure out whether it's because he's unfamiliar with affiliate marketing and needs to have a better grasp on what it is, or if there is some other reason for his resistance. If his response is "I just have a tiny list, so I don't think I could help," remind him of the benefits for his subscribers, and, if the product is being sold, that every single sale he makes will generate revenue that's all "found money." Your potential affiliate may also be reluctant to participate because she's received feedback from subscribers asking for less advertising and fewer promotions. If that's the case, ask whether you can follow up later with the same product or perhaps a different one, or better yet, ask if you can provide a content-rich article, at the conclusion of that article, which sales pitch with a "softer sell." Be open to tailoring your offer for any particular affiliate so that each one feels completely comfortable participating in your Internet marketing campaign.

You may think your product would be perfect for a particular list owner's subscribers, but assume that he knows his subscribers better than you do. If an e-mail list owner says, "It doesn't sound like this product would be right for my people," he could be right, but you might want to explore why he feels that way. It's possible that with a little more information from you, he might feel differently. As you probe and persevere, be light-hearted and polite. Be ready to meet any objections with respect and more information, and keep your tone friendly and enthusiastic.

People are busy, so if you contact a list owner a few times and he appears to be ignoring your e-mails, it may be that he means to get back to you but just hasn't had the time. To grab the attention of a potential affiliate, you might consider snail mailing him and sending him a bonus gift. You could send a fun doodad, an interesting bookmark or wallet-sized card with an inspirational message, cookies, or an item with your Website address on it such as a highlighter pen or notebook. You might even want to write to him with unusual stationery that ties in to product somehow.

Because finding affiliates is time-consuming, you may want to hire someone to help you, or even do your entire campaign. I choose to use an affiliate marketing company, Hasmark Services, to find partners for me, sign them up, send them copy, and manage the campaign. It makes my job easier to subcontract the work of finding affiliates! I pay 40 percent of the revenue for the product to the affiliate, keep 40 percent for myself, and pay 20 percent as a "finder's fee" to Hasmark.

In fact, as you launch more viral explosions and get to know and even become friends with various affiliates, you might want to earn money matching up other people with affiliates. You could develop a niche and a second business doing Internet marketing. Note, however, that if you want to hire a middle man to sign up affiliates for you, you will have to set up the shopping cart to pay two tiers of commissions, one to the affiliate and one to your middle man. (Not all shopping-cart services allow you to do this, however.)

Infuse Your Internet Marketing Campaign With Excitement!

If you have a product you're selling, you may want to offer a reduced price for a limited time only in order to elicit excitement and a strong response. I've seen successful Internet marketing campaigns built around overstocked or close-out items, for instance. People are often excited by the prospect of getting a good deal for the short time it's available. You can also make yours a "low-price introductory offer available for a limited time."

To give people a greater incentive to check out what you're offering, consider including free bonus gifts. Throughout the book, I've suggested that you create information-based eProducts you can sell or give away, and if you have several that you've produced, you have a nice collection of bonus gifts you can use to make your campaign, or a partner's campaign, more attractive. In addition to audio files and eBooks, your bonus gifts might be short documents such as forms or checklists that people will find useful, a screensaver, or just about anything that's downloadable.

One advantage to having several free bonus gifts available to offer people is that, should you be approached to become an affiliate and participate in someone else's viral explosion, you'll be able to help him by offering to let him use your free bonus gift as a giveaway to anyone who buys his product. So, let's say Bob Proctor approaches me to partner with him in his campaign for a DVD set he's selling. I offer him a free bonus gift that he can give away to purchasers, providing them with a greater incentive to buy. And let's say Bob also partners with a fellow named Tom Richards, and one of Tom's subscribers goes to pick up those bonus gifts and is intrigued by my list of 21 distinctions of wealth. He retrieves the download of the list and decides to sign up for my newsletter, and buy my book *The 21 Distinctions of Wealth.* All this happens because I've been generous in offering free, valuable bonus gifts for Bob to use in his campaign. I don't even know Tom, but he's just sent me a fan, follower, and customer!

Tip

If your affiliates are due revenue, pay them on time. Their help has been extremely valuable to you. Show them your appreciation by sending them their money as soon as possible, and keep meticulous records to ensure you don't overlook anyone or accidentally delay payment. Always, always thank your affiliates profusely for their help and their belief in the value of your product!

Make Your Campaign Go Viral!

As I mentioned before, some people may even receive a pitch for your product from more than one source, which is good because if people hear about something more than once, they're more likely to pay attention and to decide to buy the product. When people hear a message more than once, it's more likely to stick with them. If you get an e-mail offer to purchase a product that interests you, you might intend to check it out but get distracted and forget about it. If you receive another e-mail promoting the same product, you are likely to say, "Oh, that's right, I did want to check that out!" and follow through on going to the Website. That's a reason to focus on partnering with as many list owners as possible and don't worry about exactly how many people you reach or whether they might receive your offer more than once. Just get that message out there!

Also, if you are selling a book, doing a viral explosion on one particular day can launch you onto a best-seller list, which very well may capture the attention of book buyers and people who work in the book publishing industry. However, you can set up your Internet marketing campaign so that people do the e-mails within the space of a week or so. The idea of a viral explosion, however, is to make a big splash at once rather than have all your sales dribble in, and to generate a sense of excitement and urgency. People take notice when a dozen of the people they're following on a social media site are all posting about a product on the same day. They pay attention when a book suddenly is at the top of the best-seller list. That's why my advice is: Consolidate your efforts and make your Internet marketing campaign a viral explosion!

And as you venture into affiliate marketing, remember to enjoy the process. It's a lot of fun, plus you'll make some great friendships.

So, are you ready? Let's get to the specifics about how to produce a product to sell or give away!

Chapter 8

Set Up a Website and Build a Subscriber Base

A Website is a crucial tool for building a business, so if you don't have one already, you'll need to design and launch one as soon as you can. And if you already have a Website, remember, there's always room for improvement. You might want to add a new feature, such as a blog, which can involve a minimal amount of work thanks to new ways of spreading the news about recently posted *blog pieces* (I'll explain more about that in this chapter). But the most important improvement you can make is to start an e-mail subscriber list if you don't already have one. Invite visitors to sign up on your home page and elsewhere on your site. Provide them with an obvious, prominently displayed e-mail sign-up box.

The reason you want to start and constantly build an e-mail subscriber list is that it's a remarkably powerful tool for promoting your brand, business, and products. A subscriber list contains e-mail addresses and names of people who have already expressed an interest in your business. It's the perfect audience for any future messages you wish to send out, or products you wish to sell or give away. And it's a vehicle for promoting your brand.

You can maximize the effect of any viral explosion by giving people who learn of your launch the opportunity to sign up for future e-mailings from you. At the end of Chapter 9, I'll give you some ideas for how you can further promote your e-mail subscriber list and your Website, but for now, let's take a look at the basics of how to construct the powerful promotional tools of Websites, blogs, subscriber lists, and e-mail newsletters.

Your Website

It used to be that you could get away with a Website that served as an online calling card or advertisement and rarely offered new information. If you included content that was unusually useful, people might tell others about your site and you'd attract many first-time visitors, but after that, people wouldn't come back. Still, because Websites were mostly advertisements for offline businesses, owners figured it didn't matter if anyone returned to see what was new on the site. Now we all recognize the importance of making a Website engaging, exciting, and worth revisiting. A Website can also become a meeting place for a community, where people can participate in creating the content of the site and post their own ideas, opinions, and questions. Once you have avid fans of your site and you're clear on what their interests are, it will be easier to find appropriate advertising affiliates and envision products you can sell to an audience of followers you now know well.

To start a Website, you'll need a domain name.

Domain Names

For your Website's domain name, choose something easy to type and remember. You don't have to reserve every variation on the name of your site, but try to have it end in .com if you can. Designations such as .net, .tv., .edu, .org, .info, .us, and .biz are less desirable because people still expect to go to a .com to reach a business site. Often you can receive a discount on your order if you commit to more than one domain name, so consider changing the words slightly or buying up the .net version as well as the .com version (although I haven't done this, I know others have).

I don't suggest using a dash or underline, as people are likely to forget to use them. So, for instance, let's say you wanted to buy YummyDinners.com, but it's taken, and you haven't yet named your company. If the site name is not being used (check by going to *www.yummydinners.com*) you might approach the owner of YummyDinners.com and ask if she's willing to sell you the site name. If she's not, or the price is too high, or the domain name is already in use, think of a variation on it. You might buy SuchYummyDinners.com, and perhaps the slightly less desirable SuchYummyDinners.net. Either is a better choice than Such-Yummy-Dinners.com or Such_Yummy_Dinners.com. You can always link sites to each other, so you could buy TheSensationalDinners.net and have it redirect to your main site, TheSensationalDinners.com. And if there's a common typo, you could buy up that mistyped domain name and have it redirect to your site: For example, goaddy.com redirects to godaddy.com.

You don't need to instantly decide on all the extras when you reserve a domain name, although often the sites that allow you to register them will run a hosting special that will save you money if you know you want them to host the site on their server (A *host* provides you with the *server*; that is, the "place" on the Web where your Website exists. Many Websites can share the same server.)

Website Design

A Website can be set up using software from your hosting company, templates available online (often, for free), or with the help of a Web designer (who can work from a template or create a custom design). Often, Web designers will charge you less money if you're willing to give them all the copy and graphics for all the pages and specific ideas, because this makes their job easier. I have seen some very professional-looking, well-designed sites that cost the business owner next to nothing to construct.

Before you begin to design a site on your own or work with a Web designer, have some fun surfing! Find sites that you especially like—maybe one has graphics that you find very attractive and energizing, and another is extremely easy to use even though it has a lot of content. Who knows? Maybe you'll get an idea or two from the design of the site of your favorite musical artist or an author you highly admire. Pay attention to what elements of that site work for you, and borrow the ideas for your own site, whether it's a color, a way of laying out your products so that people are instantly drawn to them, or something else. You might even e-mail the Web designer who worked on a site you particularly like (there's often a link on the site itself) and ask if he or she would be willing to design a site for you.

If you're going to work with a Web designer, be sure to ask if he'll typically be available to do simple text updates the same day you request them or if he can teach you to do it yourself. Although you can usually take your time with changing design elements such as a logo or banner, you don't want old information lingering on your site, such as information about events that you did last week, last month, or worse, last year! Also, you may need to announce something quickly. Imagine you just received an invitation to appear on a major television talk show in two days to talk about your brand and message. You want that information on your site, pronto!

The look of your site should reflect your brand and be visually engaging for the visitor, and the navigation needs to be a no-brainer for a first-time visitor—and I do mean a no-brainer. Don't make people think! For instance, if there's a search box on your site, put it on the upper right with the little magnifying glass icon. Have you ever walked up to a door that says PUSH and found yourself pulling? Yes, the word's right there for you to see, but by the time you read "push" and become conscious of what it means, you're already yanking at that door handle and thinking, "What the heck is wrong here?" There are actually ways to create visual cues within a Website design that tell a person's subconscious to "push" or "click here to access the shopping cart" without someone having to use his noggin. Give your visitor cues such as a magnifying glass and a shopping cart icon and you'll free up her brain to do more important things, like check out your products, your blog, and so on!

As you design your site, the foremost questions in your mind should be:

~ Why would someone want to come to my site?

~ What experience do I want him to have when he gets there?

~ Why would a visitor to my site want to recommend this site to others?

~ Why would a visitor want to come back to my site on a regular basis?

As you design the pages, keep in mind the old real estate rule: *location, location, location.* Your Main Street storefront window is your home page. As soon as a visitor arrives, he should get a sense of what he'll find on this site and why he should stay and check it out. Sometimes you have only a second or two to grab people's attention, and the same amount of time to keep it!

Make sure your visitor is immediately aware of the opportunity to sign up to receive future mailings from you. You may want to have a few sentences welcoming the visitor and explaining how this site can serve her needs, or you may have a very short welcome video that she'll be able to view by clicking on it. I don't recommend that welcome videos be set to play automatically, because:

~ It can be jarring for the visitor who doesn't expect it.

~ It may irritate the person who has already viewed it on a previous visit.

~ A video can knock your visitor offline if his Internet connection is not a very good one.

~ If he's surfing the Web at work he might not appreciate alerting the entire office to his surfing with a big bold "WELCOME TO MY WEBSITE!" booming out of his computer's speakers!

Make your welcoming text or video short, concise, and inviting, and change it now and again.

Feature your services and products prominently on your site. You might dedicate space on the front page to what you're currently promoting. If you have multiple services and products, group them as if they were on a dessert table at a catered party. Make it yummy! And if you have a "look" to your packaging, use it on your site.

When you label your tabs for the other pages on the site, use words that people will instantly understand, such as "Contact" and "Services." And watch that overall, you keep the look of your site visually interesting but not so busy that it's overwhelming to the eye. Always use highly readable universal typefaces such as Arial and Times New Roman, and plenty of white space, graphics, and bullet points.

Put the Home Page tab on the left if the tabs are listed horizontally, and on the top if they're listed vertically, so people can get back to that home page easily. And make sure that when a cursor rolls over a live link, the color changes. Live links should always be obvious, and their color should be consistent (studies have shown that people automatically assume that words in a blue typeface are links, so that's a good color to use).

You have plenty of room for creativity when designing a site, but always keep in mind your ultimate goal: to make it an efficient tool to inform and engage your visitors, gather e-mail list subscribers, and promote yourself, your brand, your products, and your message.

Keep Your Website Fresh

My Website designer, Fernando Martinez of 3da.com, likes to say that a Website is like a bowl of fruit: If you don't change it regularly it's not going to be very attractive. You don't want fruit flies buzzing around your site! People want a reason to come back to visit—and so do search engines. Update your site's look once in a while, and regularly add information (particularly to the front page) in order to encourage multiple visits and to signal search engines to rank it again.

One way to easily alter your site is to connect it to a blog and tease the blog piece on the front page of your site: Include the first sentence or two and a link to the rest of the blog. You can also put social networking status updates and posts on your front page, and rotate quotations, announcements, and photographs. On holidays, you might add to your site some visual elements that are appropriate for the season. And think about injecting a little humor or entertainment, such as a small piece of humorous animation or a funny or inspiring quote.

Blogs

Blogs (short for "Web log") are easy to set up and can be time-consuming to keep up, but thanks to social networking sites, newsletter software, and RSS feeds, you don't have to post blog entries daily or every other day to encourage people to regularly visit your blog. You can use these tools for notifying people that you've posted a new piece.

If you're short on ideas for a blog piece, you might fashion one from a recorded interview or teleseminar you did in the past. A transcription service makes it easy to turn audio into text that you can cull from and edit. You can also do a video blog entry if you've got the right equipment. Many newer computers include an easy-to-use video camera built into them. You might also post links to articles or other blog pieces you find interesting and simply add a few comments of your own and invite readers to ring in with their opinions. People love to share stories and talk about themselves. End your blog piece with a request for their stories and experiences, and watch how quickly they respond! Blogs and social media posts don't have to be brilliantly written or deeply insightful, but they do have to add value to your site, whether it's humor and entertainment value, inspiration, information, guidance, or some thought-provoking questions that will encourage readers to dialogue with you.

Communities and Forums

It's helpful to foster a sense of community on your Website, although nowadays, you can do it via a blog on your site, where people can interact, and comments you invite on social media sites. You don't have to have forum software to get conversations going among your followers. In the offline world, we go to conventions, conferences, and group meetings not just to acquire information or learn about new products and services that offer us benefits, but to meet people with similar interests. Find ways to help your followers interact with you online.

Some sites are very much driven by their forum feature, but if you do use this Website element, be sure to monitor it for any posts that might disturb or offend other readers. The same is true of your "wall" on a social networking site, where people can write whatever they choose. Be aware of what people are posting and delete any entries you'd prefer not to have on your wall, but try to keep the conversation going and your followers engaged.

Some sites require a login ID and password to access regions of the site, and you may want to do this if you're providing a moderated forum for discussion and want to offer people the opportunity to maintain anonymity. PegMcColl@gmail.com may want to register as P283, for instance, so she can post freely without worrying that someone doing a search for her name using a search engine will quickly be able to access her post. Be sure that your software for logins allows people to easily order and receive a reminder of their password and login ID, and make it easy for them to change the password, too. Always make it as easy as possible for people to use your site.

Begin to Build Your E-mail Subscriber List

An e-mail subscriber list starts with the people who have e-mailed you for more information about your brand, products, and services. However, for each person who actually contacts you, there are many more who visit your site, whose e-mails you'll want to add to your subscriber list. Make sure you have an e-mail signup box on your Website's home page and the contact page, as I've said, and think about putting it on *every* page of your site. Design the sign-up box simply so anyone will spot it immediately and be able to fill it out easily.

Provide people clear information about what your new potential subscriber will be signing up for, and promote the benefits of subscribing. If you ask visitors to "Sign up here to receive future e-mailings," some people may be inclined to do so after they've browsed the site a bit (that is, if they haven't forgotten about that sign-up box, which is why you place it on several different pages on your site!). If you promise your would-be subscribers that they will "start to receive our helpful newsletter with practical tips," that offers a little more obvious value and sounds a little more attractive. However, visitors will be even more eager to subscribe if they know they'll receive "special discounted offers and valuable practical tips," "a free 12-page eBook delivered to your e-mail inbox," or "a free 3-part eCourse." Describe what they'll receive, emphasizing the benefits of becoming a subscriber.

Alex Carroll is a former courier driver who was successful at beating 80 percent of his traffic tickets, and he wrote a book called *Beat the Cops: The Guide to Fighting Your Traffic Ticket and Winning.* At his Website, *www.cleandrivingrecord.com*, you can sign up for a very practical newsletter indeed: Each week, you receive an excuse that a driver has successfully used to beat a speeding ticket! Now, many people want to know how to avoid speed traps and get out of paying hundreds of dollars for a speeding ticket (not to mention having their automobile insurance increased as a result of receiving points on their driver's license), so Alex Carroll was able to garner quite a lot of media attention for his site, his e-Books, and his newsletter. Whenever he was interviewed, he asked people to visit his site where they could find free tips that would help them "beat the cops." Once people got to his site and saw that he truly was offering valuable tips, they would buy other books and sign up for his newsletter. Where does Alex get so many valuable tips? Some are ones he's used, and others are successful excuses people submitted to him in the hopes of winning a free book (and, of course, helping others "beat the cops"). What sort of clever newsletter might you create for subscribers? And is there a way you can get others to voluntarily submit ideas you can use for future issues of your newsletter?

When offering an e-mail sign-up, it's a good idea to ask your subscriber for only a minimum amount of personal information. Most people don't want to type in their entire name and address, phone number, birthday, location, and an explanation of "how you heard about us" on a newsletter sign-up, and you don't really need all that data anyway. Ask for their e-mail address and first name (that's so you can personalize e-mails using your newsletter service's software). If you want more information in order to track what your subscribers do, who they are, and where they live, give them an incentive for providing the extra information. For instance, you might tell them that you're asking for their birth date so that you can send them a greeting and a free gift on their special day.

When you set up your e-mail sign-up box, *always* include a promise never to sell that person's e-mail address to a third party. This will reassure your subscribers and increase the number of people who sign up. Some sites offer people the opportunity to sign up for multiple newsletters, but if you do that, you might not want to set it up so that people have to opt *out* of newsletters. I suggest you let subscribers opt *in* to receive more material from you so they only get newsletters they expressed an interest in. In fact, you should always make it easy for people to unsubscribe from your newsletter. And you might want to create a box for comments they'll access when they unsubscribe, where you can say, "We're sorry to see you go!" and include the question, "May we ask your reason for unsubscribing?" This might help you gather some ideas on how to make your newsletter even more valuable to subscribers.

Creating and Maintaining Newsletters

Commonly, people will tell me that they've had a Website for years and the main reason they've never collected e-mails is because they feel obligated to produce a regular newsletter to send out to those who signed up to receive "further information." The good news is that you do *not* have to commit to a weekly or biweekly newsletter to build a subscriber base. However, you may want your newsletter software program to immediately acknowledge their sign-up with an auto responder. And you will need to commit to sending them something of value fairly regularly.

If you don't send out newsletters often, you might want to consider creating a simple eCourse that you set up to be automatically delivered to new subscribers throughout the course of several days. It could consist of introductory or overview information about your core topic of expertise, or a series of practical tips and strategies they'll find of use. By offering a free eCourse, you're providing value to your subscribers right away. This will make it easier to retain subscribers who might sign up, forget all about you, and then, a month later, receive a newsletter from you, mistake it for spam, and unsubscribe. Give them something valuable quickly and they'll remember why they signed up in the first place.

Your newsletter should offer information, but don't feel you must write a long essay or provide a magazine with many articles. Some highly successful newsletters will start with a few sentences about what the newsletter owner is doing or experiencing, and then launches it into less personal information. That might consist of four short but useful tips on how to do something, or perhaps a description of a trend you're seeing in the industry and a link to an article that explains more. The newsletter might simply contain a greeting and a promotion for a product created by the list owner or someone else. Another way to provide value is to include a short interview with someone else who has valuable information your subscribers will enjoy receiving.

By building a subscriber list, you are committing to provide value to your followers. The value in one e-mail you send out may be that it contains an offer you think they'll appreciate. In another, it may be some words of wisdom from you, or a reminder of upcoming events you're hosting, from workshops to teleseminars. Newsletters can also contain links to articles you feel will be helpful for your followers, inspirational quotes, powerful poems, inspiring videos, or provocative questions that will get them thinking and even interacting with you via social media or your Website forum. My friend Debbie Ford created a powerful film called *The Shadow Effect*, which explores the challenge of accepting all the aspects of ourselves, even the ones we're not fond of. She recently realized that a current big news story everyone was talking about was very closely related to the topic of her movie and her books. She sent her subscribers an e-mail with a short essay in which she evaluated the news event in light of "the shadow effect," and it touched a nerve. People began forwarding it, the essay reappeared on one of the most popular blogs in the world, and it drove up interest in Debbie and her work. Keep an eye out for news items and events that arouse people's interest in a big way, and chime in with an essay or commentary that you can post on your blog and send to your e-mail subscribers. Maybe you'll set off a viral explosion!

Newsletter Service Providers

Most newsletter services have many useful features, such as the ability to personalize e-mails in the subject line, greeting, and text, or to choose what time they're sent, or to send an e-mail in plain text or HTML. Usually, you can automatically include elements that remain the same from newsletter to newsletter, such as your logo, your signature, or a legal disclaimer at the end. You can often track whether your recipients have forwarded the e-mail to someone else or clicked on a link embedded in it, which helps with market research and with tracking affiliate sales. In fact, even though your newsletter may go out with an embedded link for forwarding to a friend, you might want to make a point of noting at the end of each newsletter "Did you find this information helpful? If so, please consider forwarding it to a friend!"

Although newsletter services are usually very easy to work with, be sure that every time you send an e-mail, you send a copy only to yourself first so that you can preview it and proofread it before it's sent to everyone on your list. It only takes a minute to do so and ensures that your newsletter is the very best it can be.

There are several reliable newsletter services, and most charge a sign-up fee as well as a fee based on the number of subscribers you have rather than the number of e-mails you send per month. Some of the shopping-cart Websites now offer newsletter service software as well. Whatever service you sign up for, choose one that gives you plenty of options for expansion. You may want to do one simple newsletter now, but then make them more elaborate or send out multiple newsletters in the future.

Build Your Business Via Your Subscriber Base

Electronically delivered newsletters can be highly effective for building your business. Brian Proctor, son of Bob Proctor, created his own viral explosion a few years ago with his insightoftheday.com newsletter. Back in 2000, before it was common to send e-mails with a quote of the day, he got the idea to launch a service where people could receive a free inspirational quote every day from Monday through Thursday, and a free inspirational story on Fridays. He figured that because he would be interested in such services, others would be, too. Word-of-mouth spread like fire over the Web, and within a month, he was making money selling products to people who had signed up because he had so many subscribers. In fact, he states plainly on the sign-up page that as a subscriber, you'll receive the quotes and story, and twice a month you'll also receive special offers for self-growth products at a discount. I think it was very clever of him to spell out exactly how many offers people will receive, because they know just what they'll be receiving. I'm sure his forthrightness led to more sign-ups than he would've had if he hadn't specified the amount of *tar-geted* advertising for discounted products they'll find in their e-mail in box.

Brian then got the idea to allow people to become affiliates of the service: They can sign up to offer the service to their own clients. The inspirational quote (or story) of the day is sent to the affiliate's list of subscribers as if it were coming from her, with her signature. People who click on a link through those e-mails and purchase products are automatically signaling the shopping-cart software to note that the order came through one of the affiliate's subscribers. The affiliates are then paid a percentage of the sale.

Through time, your e-mail subscriber list will expand and contract. Please don't fret over occasionally losing subscribers. Remember, close to 1.7 billion people are using the Internet—you've got plenty of people who have yet to sign up and discover how much value you have to offer them!

~~~

With your Website up and your e-mail subscriber list created and expanding by the minute, you are primed to set off a viral explosion. And by now, you probably have some idea of what product you want to sell or give away. It's time to get to work actually producing that product and ready yourself for a launch. In the next chapter, you'll learn the details of product creation.

Chapter 9
Create Your Products

Once you have some solid ideas about the products you want to develop, you can begin the process of creating them. If you're already selling tangible products, and aren't going to be designing an eProduct at this time, I hope you'll read this chapter anyway because it will give you some ideas on how you can expand upon the product line you already offer and generate interest in your brand and business. Mine your considerable knowledge and wisdom, and you will start seeing the vast potential for eProducts you can offer to people.

I'm going to provide you with a lot of details here because I've found, in researching how to create my own products, that it's easy to save a considerable amount of money doing it yourself rather than having someone do it for you. Producing quality products isn't as difficult as I thought it would be. Technology allows you to be a movie producer, book jacket designer, and audio engineer even if you're, like me, not very technologically inclined. And I've found that if you ever get lost or stumped, you can often just go to a search engine and type in what you're looking for; you may well find it for free or very low cost. How-to information is everywhere, but I want to give you some basics and some tips that I've learned in creating my own products.

The Steps for Producing an eProduct

In a moment, I'll go into the elements you'll need to put together to create specific eProducts, but here are the basic steps of production you'll need to follow.

1. **Come up with the topic or theme.** You may want to start with an information-based product that provides an overview of your core subject, such as "How to Get Your Book Published," "An Introductory Guide to Social Media," "How to Sell Your House Quickly," or "What to Do When You're First Diagnosed With Diabetes." Alternately, you may want to zero in on a specific subtopic, such as "How to Publish Your Young-Adult Fiction Book," "Keep Your Kids Safe From Cyber Bullying," "How to Sell Your Vacation Home," or "Managing Meal Planning as a Newly Diagnosed Diabetic." Because you're an expert on the topic, you may feel there's a lot of information on the Internet about it, but you may be underestimating the demand for that information. Besides, you will give it your own spin. I'll bet if I asked the five realtors I know to give me their best advice on how to get my home ready to go on the market, the basic advice might be the same, but each of them would say something a little different in his own style. And remember, you're going to do a viral explosion so that a good chunk of those 1.7 billion people on the Internet know about *your* product.

Also, remember that the stronger someone's emotional need for certain information, the more interest he'll have in your eProduct on that topic. If someone's very eager to sell his vacation home and your brand has real credibility, or he's gotten lots of advice but nothing that he's found to be particularly helpful for his specific situation, he may be quite interested in what you have to say in your teleseminar, eBook, Webinar, or whatever. A woman whose child has just been diagnosed as diabetic and feels overwhelmed by the need to change her cooking style may receive an e-mail about your individual and group coaching package for diabetic meal planning and feel deeply relieved that she'll get personalized information from you over the phone. Then, too, as I've said, people need information in various forms and packages, and your product may be exactly what they need right now, in the form they need it.

2. **Give your product a name.** You may want to reread the section in branding on coming up with clever titles for your business as those rules can apply here. However, a product name can be longer than a brand name. Often, what works well is to have a short, provocative title followed by a subtitle or reading line that explains in straightforward language exactly what you're getting. Books use this formula often. This book's title, *Viral Explosions*, grabs your attention and is provocative, and then the subtitle explains it: "Proven Techniques to Expand, Explode, or Ignite Your Business or Brand Online." The game Monopoly, which we all remember from childhood, even has a reading line to explain exactly what it is: "The fast-dealing property trading game."

3. **Decide on the format**. As you've learned, you have a wide array of formatting options. You might make yours a downloadable product, a class, or a physical product. Decide on how your information should be divided up. For instance, you might want to present your six hours of information and guidance in a two-session teleseminar, with each session lasting for at least three hours (plus time for Q&A), or a three-session package, with each section lasting just more than two hours.

4. **Create the text for the outside packaging.** Before you write the script for your actual product, write the text for the outside packaging and find any graphics you'll need. Do searches for topics such as "free packaging design" or "package design templates," and see the Resources at the end of this book for Websites that offer high quality packaging designs you can download. Although you could create the script or outline for your product first, when you begin by generating the advertising and promotion copy, you'll be able to more sharply focus on what it is you want to say. Keep the copy benefits-oriented and use bullet points when you can, because people love to read simple lists of benefits. Also, your copy should be tailored to your audience, whether it's beginners or people who know something about the topic and are looking for more advanced, specialized information. One thing I like to use in my copy, too, is numbers—not "You'll learn about the secrets of success" but "You'll learn about the 6 secrets to success;" not "I'll teach you about the distinctions of wealth" but "I'll teach you about the 21 distinctions of wealth." Or, you might try to be a little provocative. When people hear about my product

"Relax Your Way to Wealth," it's not just appealing, it's intriguing, because we've all been told that the way to acquire wealth is to work very, very hard.

5. **Start writing.** Several types of writing are involved in creating an information-based product. First, as I mentioned, you will need to write the copy for the package itself. You may also want to write any other advertising copy before creating your actual product, such as copy for:

   ~ Your e-mail introducing yourself to e-mail list owners, telling them about your product and affiliate program.

   ~ Your e-mail that your affiliates will send out to their e-mail list.

   ~ Your landing page.

   ~ Your Website.

   ~ Your product packaging.

6. **Produce the product or get it ready to go.** Next, you'll need to create the material for the actual information-based eProduct. This could be a book, a script you'll read aloud in order to create an audio product, or an outline for your teleseminar that you'll consult as you teach. With an eCourse, you'll have to design the format and be clear on what information or guidance you'll include. If you're doing a coaching or mentoring package, determine the price and the particulars. If you're writing a book, you have to start writing it.

   Also, at this point, you may need to book time at a recording studio or video studio, or sign up for a recording service, teleseminar service, or Webinar service.

7. **Arrange for distribution.** Create any packaging you'll need and get ready for shipping or for distributing the material electronically. If you're creating an eProduct that has text, be sure to have your copyright information listed on every page in case the product gets passed around, and if you have packaging for your product, include the copyright information there. If you're going to do a teleseminar or Webinar, research service providers and learn how to work with the technology to create a smoothly running event. If yours will be a CD or DVD, find a production company or duplication service to create the physical product.

With an eProduct, storage and shipping won't be an issue, of course, but if you want to sell a physical product such as a CD set or a book, you'll need to store the products safely in a place you can access easily to do shipping—and if you'll be fulfilling the orders yourself you'll need shipping supplies.

You may be able to store your product in your house, but sometimes that's not the best idea. If you place 3,000 books, or food or other perishable items, in an unheated garage or an uninsulated attic or humid basement, they can become damaged, so you want to be sure of what you're getting and where you'll store your inventory. Do you know how many cubic feet of storage you'll need? Believe me, I didn't know how much space 3,000 books take up until I saw them in my dining room! If you're near a city, you may be able to find a fulfillment house near you that will store, pack, and ship your products for a fee (and they may offer other services as well, such as shrink wrapping, assembling, and generating bar codes). I could

have done this with my first book, but I soon realized that having all of my inventory in my home
where I could see it every day kept me motivated
to move those books from my dining room into the
hands of people who could benefit from the information between the covers!

Hiring People Who Can Help With Production

Many types of software and hardware are available today
to help you with creating your own eProducts, but even so, you
may feel the need to get a person to help you with some aspect
of production. You may not have the time, patience, or skills
at this time to use software for audio recording or editing at
home, for instance, or you may not feel comfortable writing
your own book without professional guidance.

When it comes to finding professionals, start by asking
for recommendations from others—not just from the obvious
people, but from anyone you know. A Web designer may know
an illustrator or graphic designer who can help you with your
Website banner, book jacket, package graphics, and so on. You
can also sometimes find all-in-one services as part of a service package, as I did when I worked with a company to self-
publish my first book. But you may be able to hire people with
greater skills if you find them on your own, individually. If you
would like one-to-one or small-group mentoring to help you
with your personal business plan, there are services for learning how to use software programs, how to manage a team, and
how to create products and market them effectively on the
Web (of course, that would be my specialty!).

Keep in mind that some of the most skilled professionals are so busy doing work for their regular roster of clients
and the people those clients refer their way that they rarely if
ever market themselves. So, even though you can check with

Websites that list the names of potential editors, writers, copy-editors, designers, and so on, never overlook your online and offline networks as resources for hiring people. Someone you know, whether it's a colleague or an old high-school chum you recently reconnected with on a social networking site, may be able to recommend a professional who does extremely high-quality work. I do this for my clients all the time because I'm eager to spread the word about professionals I know who provide terrific value to their customers, and I want to help out my clients so that they have the best professionals to depend on.

The Specifics of Creating Information-Based Products

Audio Products, Including Downloadable Audio Files and CDs

1. **Write your script and practice reading it.** You may find it more comfortable to work from a script rather than an outline, or vice versa. (By the way, one reason I like to work from a script is that I'll later turn the scripts into a workbook, which gives me another eProduct to offer people). There's no right or wrong way to prepare for a recording; go with what makes it easier for you to deliver your material with energy and enthusiasm. But before doing the actual recording, practice what you'll say. If you're reading from a script, you'll quickly notice if any words are difficult to pronounce or any sentences are too long or confusing, and be able to clean that up before you do the actual recording.

   If you're not comfortable with the quality of your speaking voice, you can hire someone else to record your audio product for you. Many audio books by popular authors are actually read by famous actors and actresses. If you decide to hire people to read your material for you, be sure you have a legal agreement with them that spells out how you'll pay them and what rights to the recording they maintain, if any.

2. **Plan the length.** Look at other successful models for CD products to get an idea of how long you want your product to be. When you write your script, practice it to figure out how long the material will run when you create the audio file. Typically, I'll aim at just under 60 minutes for a CD of information. A meditation CD or one containing affirmations spoken out loud may run a quarter that length. In deciding on length, look to other successful products for examples.

3. **Record at home or in a studio.** You have several choices for recording audio products. You can use home equipment and transfer the digital audio files to your computer. You can also record directly on to your computer if you're set up to do that. You can record over the phone using a service that you pay for by the hour or by the month. These services record your phone call and immediately make it available as an .mp3 file that you can upload or transfer. Finally, you can choose to record in an actual recording studio with professional equipment, and edit there or at home on your own computer if you have the right software. In a studio, the sound quality of your recording may be higher than the quality of a recording you do at home depending your equipment and software.

When deciding upon how and where to record, make sure you're not skimping on quality. Of course, if your audio product is based on a teleseminar, you won't need to do recording in a studio, but you may want to do professional editing there and dub in any sections that you weren't totally happy with; for instance, if there was a whining sound in the background in one section, or if something didn't get recorded (unfortunately, it can happen!).

I suggest you allot a little more than twice as much time to recording your audio product as it will run; that is, if it's 90 minutes of material, plan on spending three hours in the studio or working with recording software if you're editing as you go. The more you practice, the less you'll have to pay a studio. And if you're willing to take the file home and note any edits that need to be done afterward, it may save you money by not listening to the entire audio playback in the studio. Even if you edit as you go, take the time to listen to the final audio file before you press it onto a CD or offer it for download.

When you record the audio, if you tend to talk too quickly, so that your words become a little hard for the listener to distinguish, try to slow down. If you fumble a word, repeat the entire sentence to make it easier to create a smooth edit. If you speak too quickly, it can be very difficult to edit and splice the audio file without it sounding awkward in spots. Be sure to introduce upcoming topics. Say, "Now we're going to get into the subject of creating products" or read the header (for instance, "Creating Products") out loud. See what feels and sounds more natural to you, but keep in mind that these placeholders will help your listener to know where she is in the material.

You may be nervous speaking in front of the engineer, but if you keep your sense of humor about it, you can get over the nervousness quickly.

An author friend of mine says she was so nervous making her first audio that when it came time for her to say, "Hi, I'm Margo White and I wrote a book called—" she completely blanked out on the name of her book and had to fish it out of her backpack to get the subtitle right! Instead of giving into embarrassment or being angry at herself, she allowed herself to laugh, and was able to regroup and continue without any other major mishaps.

As you record, whether you're at home or in a studio, stand rather than sit, because it makes your voice stronger and convey more energy. Have water available and throat lozenges, especially if your recording session is more than two hours long. Your voice will start to sound haggard after a certain amount of time, so don't overdo it, and keep your vocal cords moist.

Use your voice expressively, and give yourself the freedom to gesture and use facial expressions. Again, don't be shy or flustered if an engineer is watching or you're at home and your dog is looking at you in confusion about who you're speaking to! Turn up the volume on your emotions—you'll make a more engaging recording. Make sure your voice conveys your passion and your belief in the information and advice you're giving.

4. **Add music if you like.** It's a nice finishing touch to have music to introduce and end the audio, and perhaps in breaks between sections. Some music software programs let you access copyright-free audio clips and even create some of your own electronically, so you don't have to be able to play an instrument. You can also download copyright-free or *rights ready* (free) music on the Internet to use in your recordings.

5. **Begin the duplication process.** The professionals at a CD-duplication house will create breaks in the material at logical places every few minutes or so, insert smart names for the CD and maybe even for the tracks themselves, burn the CDs, and create a label to imprint on them. You can spend a few hundred dollars to purchase a CD duplicating machine to use in your home and do all of this as well, but keep in mind that burning CDs and DVDs can be very time-consuming if you're doing them one at a time on your computer. If you do decide to create the actual CDs or DVDs yourself, you can also go online to get templates for the labels, or even purchase them at an office supply store.

6. **Create the packaging or image and copy for the product, if need be.** If you'll be printing CDs, design the paper insert for the CD case and the outer packaging. If you're doing an audio download, you may not need to have graphics, because no packaging is involved. Several Websites allow you to access copyright-free graphics (check the list in the Resources section). Always run a *proof* before you commit to artwork: what looks great on screen might look very different when you see it on the package. The original artwork I'd chosen for my *Magnet for Money* CD package looked great to me when I saw the digital image on the Internet, but when the products arrived, the image of a man holding out his arms as the sun rises looked much darker than I'd thought it would. When I went back to print more copies later, I chose a more vibrant piece of art with gold coins, and learned my lesson: Ask to see a proof before you sign off on packaging.

To write the descriptive copy on the package, look at other commercially sold CDs and see how many words they used and what the formula is for the packaging copy. You might want to include a bullet-point list of benefits, an endorsement, and a tagline. It can also be effective to include a problem and solution ("Do you have trouble getting your teen to open up and discuss what's going on in her life? At last, here's the secret to improving the communication between you and your preteen or teenager"). You can always hire a copywriter to do this for you if you're really struggling, but if you look at successful formulas, it's not that difficult to identify the elements you need to create.

Video Products, Including Video Files and Videos on DVD

You don't have to be Steven Spielberg to make a movie anymore, thanks to the inexpensive equipment and software for video production now available. A simple "flip camera" can cost you a few hundred dollars, and editing software is inexpensive.

If your information is strongly dependent on visuals, particularly demonstrations of techniques, a video may be the right eProduct for you. Or you may choose to make promotional videos that can bring your products to life. One of my favorite promotional videos is one I did with my dog, Pablo, promoting my book *Be a Dog With a Bone*. Pablo has never taken acting lessons, but he was a natural (the software that made his lips move helped!). For a promotional video, you can film people offering their glowing endorsements of you, or you can introduce yourself, talk about your product and its benefits, and demonstrate how you can apply the information and advice you're offering. You might also want to create a welcome video for your Website, in which you greet your visitors and introduce yourself.

Just as with recording an audio product, when you create a video, rehearse your performance. However, be careful not to over-rehearse it because you don't want to seem stiff or bored. Keep your energy up! If you have someone you know well operating the video camera and you don't attempt to do anything too fancy, beyond the basic camera recording skills an amateur will have, you may find yourself more comfortable on camera than if a professional you don't know were filming you. Then again, some professionals are experts at putting people at ease on camera. Don't be shy about asking for whatever it is you need to feel more comfortable on camera. If the chair you're sitting in makes you feel confined, or the wind blowing against your face as you film outdoors is distracting you and making you nervous, don't try to hide your discomfort. Tell your "director" so he can help you solve the problem. Before you hire someone to film you, ask to see other work he's done with ordinary people as the "performers" and let him know you're a beginner and may need a little help working out any jitters.

Shoot any footage you know you'll need, but feel free to incorporate photographs, video, and animation you own or can buy the rights to that will help you illustrate your ideas.

Much of the advice for creating audio products applies here as well. Work with software at home, a studio, or a combination of the two, and pay attention to quality. Consider using a duplication house or production company, and make sure your packaging is ready to go before you start selling the product.

Teleseminars and Webinars

To create a teleseminar or Webinar, decide on your theme or topic, come up with a compelling name for the course, and begin to create the content. Work from a script or an outline, whichever makes you feel most comfortable, and sketch out your plan for how much time you'll spend speaking on any particular topic. Again, rehearsal is a good idea, whether it's rehearsing with your outline or script or practicing with the equipment and technology for a few minutes so that you start your seminar feeling confident and ready to go. And when you do present your teleseminar or Webinar, be sure you leave plenty of time for questions and answers at the end.

You can increase the value of your teleseminar or Webinar if you allow your listeners to access the recording at a later date. And as I've mentioned, you can create an audio product from the seminar, which you can then sell. Sometimes, the issues and questions that come up in the Q&A will plant seeds for future products.

Decide on the total number of people you'd like to attend your seminar and find a service that provides the software you'll need (see the Resources section). In general, as I write this, the services for teleseminars tend to allow you to have more attendees than do the services for Webinars, but that may change. Be sure you feel comfortable with the amount of attendees you can have when you use that service and check whether there's an option for upgrading the service should your viral explosion yield even more attendees than you expected. And while you'll announce to your attendees the specific times they'll attend, call into the phone line or log into the Webinar service at least 15 minutes in advance so that you'll have time to welcome people as they call in; typically, these services will instruct callers to announce themselves once connected. It's nice to be able to say "Hello Sam! Glad to have you join us!" before "class" starts. Also, book an extra 15 minutes or so in case you run long, because the call will automatically end at the designated time.

If you want to host a teleseminar, as mentioned previously, choose a service that will allow you to open up the phone lines at some point so attendees can ask questions or chime in with suggestions for each other. Of course, you don't have to use this feature if the teleseminar ends up having so many attendees that it would be chaotic to open the phone lines, but it's good to have so that people can ask questions over the phone rather than e-mail them to you as you're speaking. With a Webinar, an Internet chat room where they can type their questions is part of the service, and sometimes you can even have your group break out into subgroups that can carry on another discussion in a chat room.

While I'm running a teleseminar, I have my e-mail program open so I can see if someone is e-mailing me a question, because the conference line is in presentation mode and the participants are currently muted so they can't be heard. If it's a query about some aspect of the topic I won't acknowledge it until we get to the Q&A section, but it's possible that I might receive a message about a technological problem with the teleseminar that I need to address. It's only happened to me once, but apparently my presentation line went dead and I had no idea that my attendees couldn't hear me. Had I been accessible by e-mail (or instant messaging), I could have received a message from one of my students telling me that I couldn't be heard.

You can host a teleseminar or Webinar without any support materials if you like, or you can incorporate other technologies and software, such as Microsoft PowerPoint presentations, Word documents, Adobe.pdf documents, and Microsoft Excel spreadsheets. Create these ahead of time. If you've never worked with the service before, or incorporated these multimedia elements, I suggest you practice with it. Do a dry run in which you have some friends call in to be sure you know how to work the phone lines and switch to a different medium on a Webinar.

eBooks and Traditional Books

As I've said, one of the best things about electronic books, or eBooks, is that you can make them any length or format you like, based on what makes most sense given the information you want to convey. You can write an eBook on whatever topic you like.

On the other hand, if yours is a nonfiction book, a publisher will require you to submit a *book proposal* that will give its decision-makers the information they need to determine if your book is a good investment for them. The book proposal is a document that describes the book that will be written, provides a writing sample, and includes marketing information that will persuade the publisher to believe that the book will sell well. Even if you've already written the book, a publisher will want a book proposal from you.

The editor or editors in a book-publishing house will edit your manuscript and provide you with some guidance to make changes to improve it, but they won't do substantial editing, so you may need to hire an editor or ghostwriter to help you before you submit the book, and you may want to hire one to help you create a book proposal. You may decide that you'll do the writing and hire an *editor* to fix any structural problems and *line edit*; that is, fix your grammar, punctuation, and spelling, smooth transitions within the text, and make sure all your word choices work beautifully. Or, you may decide to hire a *writer* to interview you, review anything you've already written, do any research that's required to make the book stronger, and write the actual book. If the writer is credited on your book, she's called a *cowriter*, but if she isn't, and remains anonymous, she's called a *ghostwriter.*

If you choose to self-publish or use a print-on-demand service, you'll need to hire professionals to help you, including an editor, possibly a ghostwriter, a book designer, a jacket designer, and a printer/binder, which will cost you money.

Some companies offer a package in which they provide all of these professionals, and that's the avenue I took with my first book. Later, I realized I could have found those professionals on my own and saved myself some money. With social networking so commonly used now, it's easier than ever to find a professional via your own network. You can also use search engines, or find people through job sites such as freelancer Websites.

Finding a Traditional Publisher for Your Book

Should you decide you want to convince a traditional book publisher to publish your book, you will almost certainly need a literary agent. Editors are so busy that they use literary agents to screen their submissions, and the majority won't look at your project if it isn't represented by a literary agent. Literary agents typically require that you pay them 15 percent of your earnings on any sales they make on your behalf. An agent's personal connections to top editors, knowledge about the publishing industry, and ability to negotiate the best possible contract for you can well justify your paying her that 15 percent.

Most often, the author comes to the literary agent rather than the other way around. But sometimes, a person's platform is so impressive that he's approached by a literary agent or even an editor before he even has a book idea. You could make this happen by focusing on building your platform and creating viral explosions to sell other products before deciding to write a book.

Next, if you're working with a book publisher, the company will oversee the production of the actual book after the edited manuscript is submitted to their production department. Your job will be to make any minor changes to the text along the way and perhaps weigh in on the look of the book. If you're self-publishing, you'll need what's called a book designer or text designer who will choose a font, decide on the look of the page, and help you pick a trim size. With an eBook, it's all up to you. My one caution would be to not get too creative with the look so that people have a hard time reading it. Consult books you've enjoyed reading and notice what typefaces they use, how much space is on the page, any design elements that you find eye-catching, and so on.

As soon as you finish the manuscript, try to garner endorsements from other authors or well-known figures in your area of expertise. See the advice for testimonials in Chapter 1.

Next, you'll need to obtain an ISBN if your book is going to sell through an online bookseller or a brick-and-mortar store. Often, printer and binder services and POD services will help you with this, or you can get one on your own (see the Resources). And on the copyright page (the other side of the title page in a physical book), list the copyright in this form: "copyright © 2010 My Name." List it on the bottom of every page of your eBook as well. Simply by noting the copyright, you've protected yourself, but you should also register the book with the appropriate copyright office (see the Resources). And if yours will be a physical book, you'll need a printer and binder, and a fulfillment house or space to store and ship it.

eCourses

First, decide on the topic or theme of your course and give it a name. Then sketch out or outline your material, dividing it into lessons. If you're giving away a free eCourse to build your subscriber list, you may want to keep it simple and make it a three- or four-part course delivered by e-mail on a regular basis (perhaps one every three days until all have been received by the subscriber). Most newsletter services make it easy for you to deliver an eCourse in this way.

However, if you want to sell your eCourse, you probably want to make it longer and more involved, perhaps requiring homework. The quality of writing and editing is not as important as it is with an eBook or a physical book, but you will have to have strong content.

In general, because some people are visual learners and some people are audio learners, I like to have both text and audio versions of my eCourse material. For example, I'll set it up so that purchasers can download an .mp3 file as well as transcripts in the form of a .pdf and a Microsoft Word document (they access these on a secure Website for which I provide them a password). You don't have to type up the transcripts yourself if you use a transcription service.

Mentoring, Coaching, and Consulting Packages

Although you can simply agree to mentor or coach people on an hourly basis, and work off of a bank of hours or bill them as you go along, it's a good idea to design a package that requires them to commit to working with you a certain number of hours.

Choose a name for your consulting or mentoring package, determine the frequency of the sessions and the length, such as 30 minutes one-to-one once a week with a 60-minute group session once a week, for a total of four weeks. Figure out how you'll answer any questions your clients have and let them know how you'll handle them. For instance, you can have an open Q&A section as part of each class, set up the package so that each individual receives a certain amount of one-to-one time with you, or agree to answer a certain number of e-mailed questions from each student as part of the package. Also, decide upon how often they can reschedule a missed session (typically, I'll allow mentoring clients to reschedule as often as they wish, providing they give me 48 hours notice).

Figure out how you will deliver your material to the group and to the individuals. You may want to use teleconferencing or a Webinar service, work over the phone, or meet with people in person.

Subscription Service

If you'd like to set up a subscription service for your customers who are seeking the information you can offer them, you can charge them by the month, the quarter, or the year. Publishers Lunch is a monthly newsletter that features a round-up of news from the book publishing industry, from deals made to job openings, and includes links to news articles on various aspects of book publishing. Subscribing also gives you full access to their Website and a free member page, and you can cancel at any time. Another business model is to allow customers to sign up for a minimal amount of money, charged to their credit card, and then auto-deduct future monthly or quarterly payments.

Protect Yourself Legally

With any product you sell or give away in which you offer advice that could be deemed legal, medical, or psychological, or if you make promises about achieving particular results using your program, you should include a legal disclaimer. You can look at other products for examples of what you might include, although the disclaimer itself is protected by copyright law, so you'll have to come up with your own variation on it. You may want to consult a lawyer to help you write a disclaimer.

~~~

Now that you know all the elements of a successful viral explosion, it's time to figure out your plan for your launch. You'll have to work out a budget and a schedule, and learn the art of creating the all-important landing page, which will give people all the details about your offer.

Chapter 10

Launch Your Viral Explosion!

Are you ready to launch? Have you set a date? Social media expert Kenneth Yu says that people more often do things out of desperation than inspiration, and that's why deadlines work. I agree! If you want to be sure you get done everything you need to do to launch a viral explosion, set a deadline for your launch. I've had clients do successful launches in as little as three weeks, although the amount of time you'll need depends on a several factors.

I've been doing viral explosions for years, and I know all that's involved, and have many affiliates I work with, so I will sometimes plan a launch for three or four weeks away. If you're starting out, I suggest you create a checklist of all the elements involved in your launch and estimate the time involved in creating the landing page, producing your product (or getting ready to host a teleseminar or Webinar), and signing up a large number of affiliates. Write out on a calendar what you feel is a reasonable schedule to do everything on your list (some of which you may have already done or decided you'll skip for now):

~ Create a Website.

~ Sign up with a newsletter service and begin collecting e-mail addresses of subscribers and sending them information regularly (start to do this via your Website).

Then, estimate how long it will take for you to take all of the 8 elements you'll need to launch a successful viral explosion:

~ Gather any downloadable eProducts that you want to offer as **bonus gifts** to people who respond to your Internet marketing campaign (more on that in a moment).

~ Set up **shopping-cart** software (more on that in a moment, too; you can do it in a matter of minutes).

~ Sketch out a **budget** for the project.

~ Create a **landing page** and test it so that you know it's ready to use and working perfectly.

~ **Create your product.**

~ **Sign up affiliates.** Identify them, write up your e-mail to them so that it's ready to be personalized and sent out, then start signing them up! Keep records of who you're contacting so you stay organized. Write up brief pitch letters for them to send out to their people, generate affiliate IDs for them, and check in with them every few weeks to let them know how the campaign is going and gently remind them of what they'll need to do (and what day is launch day).

~ **Launch!**

When you choose your launch date, think about whether you might tie the launch into a noteworthy date or an upcoming season or event. If your products have a theme of self-improvement, you might offer them in January for the New Year. If they tie in to the desire for romance, try Valentine's Day. If they are related to helping kids do better in school, choose a September launch date. You might also do an explosion to celebrate your 50th birthday, your 10th anniversary of being in business, or some other event that people will be talking about that somehow ties into what you're offering.

Step 1: Gather Your Bonus Gifts

Whether the purpose of your viral explosion is first and foremost to sell a product, or simply to promote your brand, it's a great idea to give away lots of free bonus gifts, as I've said. You don't have to necessarily create these yourself. You can actually find online sites that let you download and distribute eBooks that are in the public domain; that is, copyright-free. You can also ask people you know to let you give away eProducts they've created. Set up a download page for people to retrieve the bonus gifts by clicking through each gift-giver's site to download the eBook, audio file, or other gift. In this way, you're helping drive traffic to their site.

> **Tip**
>
> Why not give back a little and offer to give a percentage of the proceeds from sales of your product to a charity you support? This will encourage people to participate and, even if they don't, you'll have a chance to promote that good cause.

Step 2: Set Up Your Shopping-Cart Service.

Many Websites offer you the ability to collect payments, but be sure you choose one that also allows you to calculate and track affiliate payments. Generally, they charge an annual fee for you to use the service rather than charging per transaction. Make sure your service has an auto-response feature so that as soon as your customer places an order and it is approved by you, it sends an e-mail to her verifying it. If your product is an upcoming teleseminar or Webinar, a subscription, an eCourse, or a mentoring package, the auto response should remind the customer of any details she'll need in order to access and use the product, and give her a schedule of what to expect. For instance, the e-mail might say "Class starts Monday night. Please call this number at 7 p.m. EST and be logged on to your computer." You might even set up a series of auto responses, including e-mails that say "Remember that tonight is the night of the Webinar."

You'll find Websites for my favorite shopping-cart services in the Resources.

Step 3: Plan Your Budget

Factor in:

~ production costs

~ cost of teleseminar or Webinar services, extra telephone or Internet access charges if you don't have an unlimited package with your communications provider

~ outsourcing of tasks such as package design, editing, copywriting, and Web page design

~ cost for the shopping cart service

~ any initial outlay for shipping materials (which will be reimbursed when you make sales because you'll charge for shipping and handling).

Step 4: Create a Landing Page

Buy a URL and hosting service for your lengthy, single-page Website that will contain sales copy. Then, write the copy (you'll get detailed instructions on how to do that later in this chapter) or hire someone to write it. Remember, you'll need your landing page and your product before approaching affiliates so they know you're serious about this launch. If you have a Website already, add the sales page to that existing site.

Step 5: Create Your Product (or get ready for the teleseminar, Webinar, or mentoring sessions)

You know how to do this by now. Make sure that if you're going to get help from professionals such as a writer or a videographer, you contact them early, because they may have a packed schedule.

Step 6: Approach and sign up affiliates

You learned how to do this in Chapter 6. As you sign up affiliates, add their information to your spreadsheet or file, then generate an affiliate ID for them using your shopping-cart software. Make it easy for your affiliates by doing everything for them. You've learned how to write a short pitch letter they can paste their name into and send out to their subscribers. Run the pitch letter through an online spam filter to ensure that it won't get caught in spam folders, then send them the pitch letter, the ID, and a reminder of your launch date.

Step 7: LAUNCH!

Copywriting Landing Pages

Copywriting is a skill that's as helpful for launching Internet marketing campaigns as keyboarding is for anyone who works on a computer. You could hire a copywriter to create your landing page, but it's costly to do so. I believe anyone who has minimal writing skills and is willing to look at a few sample pages (I've listed some in the Resources) and follow the guidelines here can write an extremely effective landing page.

As I've said, landing pages, sometimes called sales pages, landing pages are lengthy advertisements that are uploaded onto an URL. A simple Web page which usually is connected to your existing Website, your landing page will need a design (usually based on a template) that features selling copy, a sign-up box for your e-mail list, and several boxes for clicking through the site to purchase the product you're offering. (Note that if you decide to create a landing page even though you don't have a Website yet, you'll have to purchase a domain name and sign up for hosting services.) I'm sure you've seen landing pages in the past, although you may not realize it. Check out *www.viralexplosions.com* for an example.

A landing page sometimes doesn't allow you to order a product but instead urges you to sign up to receive more information. In this case, it's called a *squeeze page.* A squeeze page weeds out any people who are only casually interested in the product and are unlikely to buy when they get to the actual shopping cart. Higher-priced products often include a squeeze page. By requiring a sign-up for more information, you give yourself another chance to make a pitch to the customer before you announce exactly the price and format of the product.

Landing pages are *very* lengthy, as long as 40 typewritten pages. Some potential customers will actually read every single line of a landing page, but most will bounce around and read the parts that appeal to them before making the decision to order the product or leave the site. Research has shown that longer landing pages have better conversion rates, that is, a higher percentage of visitors who go on to place an order than the number of visitors placing an order on a similar landing page that doesn't contain as much text.

Landing pages are a bit like infomercials in that they are chock full of sales copy, endorsements, promises, warnings (about what will happen if you don't order), and urgings to order now because it's a limited-time offer. The formula may seem complex at first, but if you use these guidelines as a checklist, and look at other examples, I'm sure you'll see that it's not all that difficult to follow.

Here is the basic formula for your landing page, based on pages that have performed well for people in the past:

Write an attention-grabbing headline. You need a sentence that's so compelling people can't help but read further because of its strong emotional appeal.

Identify the reader's problem. To connect with people emotionally, point out a problem they're having and reach out to them with an expression of compassion and understanding. Have you ever seen a commercial for a cleaning product on television and laughed at the point where the actor is frustrated because he's scrubbing like crazy with no results, or annoyed by trying to work with an awkward tool to solve a home repair problem? The depiction may be over the top, but you don't turn away, do you? That's because we've all been there, frustrated by a seemingly simple task, so we identify with the person onscreen. Similarly, you want to tell a story on your landing page that starts by identifying a problem that your reader can relate to.

The person in the story could be the reader ("Like many people, you may be frustrated by..."), or it could be a client ("For years, I've been counseling clients who came to me because they struggled with the problem of..."), or even you ("Nine years ago, I was an unemployed single mother trying to make ends meet...."). The idea is to paint an emotional story of a journey from an annoying or upsetting problem to a deeply satisfying solution. People respond to stories of triumph over troubles. Work one into your copy, starting with the problem.

You might even use statistics that show how many other people have a similar problem, and say "You aren't alone!" in order to help the reader feel that you genuinely care about his urgent challenge.

Explain why other solutions don't work or haven't worked. On the journey from problem to solution, the person in your story surely tried some solutions that didn't produce good results. If the person in the story is the visitor to the landing site and you're trying to paint a picture of what he's going through, tell him why the other solutions he may be considering won't work for him, and warn him away from inferior products or approaches that are not going to achieve results for him. If your product or message is designed to help people develop an exercise routine, write something like, "You've heard about dangerous diet pills and you have probably been tempted to try them, but you don't have to risk your health to lose weight." The idea is to get the reader to nod and say, "Yep, that's been my experience, and those are my concerns!"

Offer a solution. At last, you can solve your reader's problem! Begin to explain what your product is and its remarkable benefits.

Insert a "Buy Now" button in several places. As soon as you've first described the product, give your reader a chance to buy it now. Insert a simple "buy now!" button that links to your shopping cart (even if what you're pitching is free eProducts, you'll need a button like this—it may say "Claim these valuable eBooks now!" or "Click here now to sign up for this free Webinar!"). Use this "buy now" or "click here now" button several times in the landing page.

Focus on benefits, benefits, benefits! Play up your product's benefits for the reader. Show people the value of what you're offering. But don't just do this with text, do it with endorsements that validate your claims and expertise.

Validate your claims and expertise. Use facts, numbers, and statistics if you can. I've seen landing pages that have screenshots of cashed checks and bank statements (with important routing numbers and personal information blacked out) to prove that someone made money using the program he's pitching.

Provide "social proof" if you can. Another way to validate your claims and expertise is to provide "social proof"; that is, testimonials from real people who have used your products or services in the past and can vouch for you. Again, include a photograph and their full name, or at the least their first initial and last names. If you can—and this is easy to do now with built-in Web cams on so many computers—ask them to provide video testimonials. Help them to describe the specific benefits of what you have to offer if they have trouble doing so. There's nothing wrong with writing their endorsement for them and getting them to agree to put their names to those words. Of course, your product may differ somewhat from what you've offered before but that's okay as long as the two are related. So, while you may not have done a Webinar before on creating effective promotional videos, your clients who have worked with you one-to-one can vouch for the value of your teaching methods and approach as well as the information you offer.

Offer a great price. Of course, you may be giving away a free product, but if you're selling something, offer your customers a good price. People love to feel they're getting a great deal. If you've offered the product before at a higher price, lower it and let them know you're only charging this lower price for a limited time. After you've built up the value of your product, announce the price that the package is worth, and try to lend some credibility to the price you're naming. For instance, you could say, "You might pay as much as $500 for just two hours of individual coaching." Point out how much money the reader might spend trying to figure out on her own how to solve her problem.

Create a sense of urgency. It's very effective to create a sense of urgency for the potential customer. Make him feel that he shouldn't hesitate and think about it some more. To get him to buy now before leaving the landing page, let him know that this is a limited-time offer, or that your stock is limited, or the offer ends on a specific day at midnight. You'll then have to make sure you do end the special offer or raise the price at some point. Otherwise, your landing page will be like those signs in shop windows in New York City that are faded by the sun because they're so old and yet claim the prices in the window are part of a "Going out of business" sale! If it's a limited offer, make it a limited offer. You can always run a limited offer again at a later point.

Anticipate any objections. People may wonder why you're giving them a deal. You might say something such as, "I'm overstocked on this product and my wife told me I have to clear out the inventory I'm storing in our home," or "I've just released this amazing new product and want to get the word out, so for a limited time, I'll be selling it for the super-low price of..." Then, too, you'll want to list even more benefits *after* naming your price. Point out the convenience of the product, or the uniqueness of it. Give more information about your reputation and include even more testimonials. It can be very effective to actually spell out the concerns the reader might be having; list them in bullet points, and respond to each one. Don't forget to insert that "Buy now" button into the copy in several places! Typical objections you can address are:

~ What makes this different from other products or offers?

~ What results can I expect? (In keeping with the FTC guidelines, be sure that you include the *typical* results; it's not enough to give an example of someone who had unusually terrific results and say "Results not typical.")

~ What is the value?

~ Are there any guarantees that this will work? (In fact, a money-back guarantee typically doubles your sales. If your product truly delivers, consider offering a guarantee.)

~ Why should I get this now?

~ What if I don't like it?

~ Who else has benefited, and how?

~ Is this person credible?

Ask a provocative question. Encourage the reader to think about her dreams and goals, to imagine that she could solve her pressing problem and make her life better in some way. Include the benefits she'll receive. For instance, you could ask a question like, "If you knew that doing just one thing today would instantly increase your personal power to blast through to your goals, receive more than $350 worth of free bonuses, and, at the same time, help your company's team to work together with efficiency and greater enthusiasm...would you do it?"

Add a bonus or bonuses. We've all heard the "reel them in" line on those late-night commercials after they announce the deal you'll be getting if you buy now; namely, "But wait! There's more! We'll throw in a free..." By this point in the commercial, you're probably itching to pick up the phone, or at least amused by how effective the pitch is to someone like you who can't think of a single reason why she needs a tube of unbelievably strong glue, or who "hates messy paint splatters" but has no intention of painting a room any time soon. Bonus gifts make people feel they're getting a bargain.

Throughout this book, I've been suggesting ways you can use freebies to draw people's attention to your brand, message, and products, and make them trust that you want to provide them with something of value. As part of your viral explosion, make sure you have at least one but preferably several more free bonus gifts. These can be eBooks and audio downloads on related subjects, subscriptions to valuable newsletters, or similar eProducts. And remember, these do *not* have to be eProducts you create. You can actually find free eBooks you can offer to people; there are Websites with dozens of them available, and even some shopping-cart Websites feature free eProducts to use in your campaigns. Do an online search and see what you can find. Also, contact potential affiliates. If I give you a free audio download I've created for you to give to your customers, they will have to come to my site to retrieve it, and once they are there, I have an opportunity to encourage them to join my e-mail list. It costs me nothing to lend you my free eProduct to use in your campaign, and it helps me by boosting my own brand's visibility.

Also, to create a sense of urgency, you can structure your offer so that the customer can only claim the bonus gifts for a limited time, whether it's on the day of the launch or for a short period.

Say it more than once. As I've said, embed your "Buy now!" button several times on your landing page. Repeat the amazing price and benefits. Remember, people don't necessarily read every word of a landing page, and in skimming, they may miss something you have to say the first time it appears in the text.

Use compelling, energetic sales language. Landing pages that work well use strong sales language. If you're a low-key person, you might feel a little uncomfortable with claims such as "you can live the life of your dreams" or "finally, the solution you've been seeking for years." Make sure your claims are truthful and your promises that the product has value are sincere, of course, but recognize that sales copy requires a certain amount of exuberance. You may have to push yourself out of your comfort zone a bit to engage people on an emotional level. If you want results, you have to infuse your text with energy. Here are some high-energy words and phrases you can use:

Discover	Easy
Free	New
Save	Results
It's here	Introducing
Finally!	At last
Proven	Like magic
Bargain	Quick
Sale	Breakthrough
Groundbreaking	Just Arrived
Now	Announcing
Imagine	What if your dreams
Exactly what you need	

Provide Clear Instructions. Your "buy now" button may say "Click here to reserve your spot!" or you might insert an explanatory sentence above it, such as, "Click below and let's get started on the path to making your dream come true." Your e-mail sign-up box should make it clear what the subscriber is signing up for, what benefits he'll receive by giving you his e-mail address. When he signs up for your list, validate his response and encourage him to keep reading about your amazing new offer. Bring his attention back to that landing-page copy.

Break up the text. Because a landing page contains a lot of words, you should break up the text to make it easier to read. Don't use so many different fonts, type sizes, and colors that you visually overwhelm the reader, but alter the look of the text for variety and use plenty of white space, bullet points, and numbered lists. Keep your sentences and paragraphs short and simple.

Checklist for your Landing Page Copy

When you're done writing your copy, ask yourself:

~ Is the heading truly catchy?
~ Does my offer have a sense of urgency or a reason to buy immediately?
~ Is the copy compelling?
~ Would I be captivated by this offer?
~ Does it make the reader want to keep reading?
~ Is it easy to understand and follow?
~ Did I add value through free bonuses or gifts?
~ Did I offer a great discounted price and show why this is a fantastic bargain?
~ Can the reader clearly see what needs to be done to buy the product?
~ Do I have social proof or endorsements that are credible?
~ Have I clearly outlined the benefits?

~~~

I hope by this point you are excited about the potential for launching your own viral explosion and eagerly jotting down ideas for yourself. I truly believe that the basic formula for this type of Internet marketing campaign can work for anyone who is willing to do the work, and can be used again and again to build a business, sell products, and get a message out to thousands and even millions of people.

As the number of Internet users continues to expand, and more and more applications, software programs, and communication devices become available, the opportunities for igniting a viral explosion will increase exponentially. So start dreaming up your next product and Internet marketing campaign, and always remember, this is all about what you can provide to others that's of value. Connect to your passion, stay in prosperity consciousness, partner with excellent people, and you'll find the sky's the limit.

More Strategies to Promote Your Newsletter, Brand, and Website

Launching a viral marketing campaign should be part of a larger ongoing strategy to promote your newsletter, brand, message, and Website everywhere. Whenever possible, launch your efforts to coincide with your viral explosion so that you have further fuel for the success of your launch. Connect with your creativity and think about the many ways you can "get the word out." Here are some ideas to start you off:

~ **Insert your site's URL into your signature line.** Embed it into the signature line of every e-mail you send, and type it in next to your signature when you post on others' blogs or review products online.

~ **Ask other list owners for help.** Request that they promote your Website and mention your newsletter to people. Ask if they'll exchange links, so that their visitors come to your site and vice versa.

~ **Buy click ads.** Choose keywords carefully to attract to your Website people who are searching for keywords related to the topic of your newsletter, brand, and business, and keep an eye on how much you're spending each day and how well various keywords are working for you.

~ **Embed your URL into your biography in articles.** Write informational articles for other people's sites, and embed a link to your Website in your short biography at the end of the article. You can submit them to free article sites, which are accessed by people who want content for their sites or newsletters.

~ **Promote your newsletter on your business card.** You can mention it on the front or the flip side of the card.

~ **Insert your Website's URL into documents and presentations.** Slip it in at the bottom of every slide in the PowerPoint presentations you make at live events, as part of teleseminars and Webinars, and as a footer on each page of any eBooks you create.

~ **Do giveaways at public appearances.** Create flyers and brochures that include your site URL and mention of your newsletter, and even print your URL on objects you hand out to people or have stuffed into goodie bags for conference attendees.

~ **Run a contest.** Contests are a great way to build your subscriber list, although you should always check your state's or area's rules about conducting contests and lotteries to be certain you're obeying the local laws. You might give away products of value to a random new subscriber who signs up by a particular date.

~ **Promote your newsletter list in social media.** Ask others to as well. Whenever you post something new on your site, or have a newsletter going out that has important information for people, post about it on social networking sites.

~ **Arrange to do interviews with the media.** Make sure that, before the radio, television, print, or online interview ends, you plug your Website and newsletter—it's easy to forget in the moment! Announce a free giveaway to entice people to visit and sign up for your e-mail list. Also, subscribe to newsletter services that feature requests from bloggers, freelance writers, and reporters looking for anecdotes and insights from experts on the topic they're writing about.

~ **Write and send out press releases.** There are many services that will send out your release for you. When you write a release, follow the standard format of other releases, but be sure to focus on the newsworthiness of your product release or message, not just the promotion. Define a problem (that's the news piece) and discuss how your product or service addresses it (that's the promotion piece). In other words, instead of simply announcing your upcoming teleseminar on helping school-age children to develop a love for reading, come up with a news-like headline with a provocative statistic about the changes in children's reading habits in recent years.

~ **Write an article, blog piece, or opinion essay on a timely subject.** Although you may have to move quickly to keep up with the news cycle, consider writing and submitting or distributing an article, blog piece, or opinion essay on a timely subject that somehow ties in to your brand, expertise, and products. Be ready for opportunities to share what you know with people who are suddenly interested in a topic that you can address.

~ **Make a promotional video.** Your video can be provocative to encourage people to check out your Website and brand, or tell an emotionally engaging story. Some people have been able to launch viral explosions with videos, especially ones that are very entertaining as commercials that gently sell a product rather than directly addressing the viewer and listing its benefits. Imagine creating a video that people love, that somehow fits in to the theme of your product and has a simple title card at the end listing your brand and Website URL.

Do you have any other ideas for low-cost, highly effective promotion? Have you launched a successful viral explosion? I would love to hear about your stories and ideas. Please share them with me and others at my Website, *www.destinies.com*!

Glossary

affiliate marketing. A marketing program or campaign that uses compensated partners to promote a product.

affiliates. Partners in marketing who agree to promote a product, often, but not always, in return for a share of the revenue generated by sales of the product.

blog. Short for *Web log*, a blog is an online journal that allows the creator to post text, video, audio, and links, and invite comments from others. A blog can be self-standing or it can be connected to a Website. "Blog" is also a verb: "I want to blog about that topic."

blog piece. An essay or comment posted on a blog.

cowriter. A cowriter shares the work of writing with another person. She receives public credit for her role (for example, if she cowrites a book, her name will appear on the cover).

cookies. Also known as *tracker cookies*, these are bits of information stored on an Internet browser that allow a Website to remember the settings it last used for the visitor. When you "clear cookies" on your browser, the information is erased. Cookies are used to record shopping-cart contents, user IDs and passwords, and other information that the visitor might want to access upon his next visit.

copyeditor. An editor whose duties include fact-checking, correcting grammar and punctuation, and proofreading. A copyeditor does less rewriting and structuring than an editor typically does, so if both an editor and copyeditor are working on a book, the editor's work will be completed before the copyeditor begins his task.

copywriter. A professional writer whose specialty is composing sales or advertising text, or copy.

e-mail subscriber list. A compilation of e-mail addresses and names of people who have contacted the e-mail list owner and agreed to be added to a list for receiving future e-mails. An e-mail subscriber list should not be confused with an e-mail list compiled by a third party, which generates *spam,* that is, e-mail communications that have not been requested by the recipient.

e-mail subscribers. People who have chosen to receive future e-mails from an e-mail list owner and provided their e-mail address and other information.

eBook. Short for electronic book, an eBook is a digital book. Although it may be in an Adobe.pdf format, for an eBook to be read on a computer, eReader, or smart phone, it must be formatted so that it can be read on that particular device.

eCourse. A series of e-mails sent to recipients to provide them with information in a sequential manner. An eCourse may also involve interaction with the students, and homework, just as with an offline course.

editor. An editor organizes, corrects, and condenses text. Editors who work at publishing houses (sometimes called *in-house editors*) or at periodicals will also have the duty of choosing material for publication, and may or may not do the actual editing of the text.

eProduct. A digital, electronic product such as an audio, video, or electronic book.

eReader. A device for displaying eBooks so that they can be read, usually handheld. Kindle and Nook are popular eReaders. A smart phone can serve as an eReader as well.

Facebook. A popular social networking site, originally created for use by college students, where people can interact online and exchange information through various means, including a personal "wall" where they and their Facebook friends can post short messages.

FTC. The Federal Trade Commission, a division of the U.S. government that regulates, oversees, and enforces rules regarding advertising and promotion in order to protect consumers.

fulfillment house. A company that offers product storage, shipping, and related services to business owners.

ghostwriter. A ghostwriter writes other people's books, articles, and reports for them and does not receive public credit for her work. The term *ghost* refers to the fact that her role in the writing is invisible to the public.

hosting service. A company that provides the bandwidth for maintaining a site on the World Wide Web. Most hosting services have their own servers and offer extra services such as Website templates and the ability to secure domain names.

information-based product. A product, or package of services, where the value lies in the information, guidance, and advice provided. A book is an information-based product. An eBook is an information-based eProduct.

landing page or sales page. A page on the Internet that is freestanding with its own Web address or that is attached to a Website or blog, a landing page contains sales copy and links.

LinkedIn. A social networking site, originally designed for professionals seeking to interact with other professionals.

Internet server. Hardware and software combined that provides users with the ability to host Websites in virtual reality. A server may be used by more than one host.

spam. E-mail or other electronic communication that has not been requested or solicited by the receiver. Spam e-mail is sometimes called "junk e-mail."

streaming. Data transfer that sends digital information in a steady "stream." Audio or video files that play using streaming software do not download to your computer when they play.

teleseminar. Short for a **tele**phone **seminar.** The presenter secures a teleconference line through a service and has attendees dial in at a predetermined time to participate in this live event.

Twitter. A social networking site where users can post very short messages called "Tweets."

viral explosion. An extremely rapid spread of information via the Internet that yields extraordinary results.

voiceover internet protocol. A service that allows people to use Internet connections to communicate in real time via audio and video. Skype is the most well-known voiceover Internet protocol.

wall. Some social media sites feature a Web page that is controlled by you, often called a "wall." Anyone who is who is part of your network can post on your wall and read the posts. You have the ability to delete posts, respond to them, or begin a dialogue and invite others to respond by posting on your "wall."

Webinar. Short for **Web**-based sem**inar.** A presentation, lecture, or workshop that's transmitted over the Internet and which allows the attendee to see the presenter, and any of her presentation materials, in real time.

YouTube. A video-sharing site on the Internet.

Resources

In addition to checking out these resources, be sure to do Web searches by keyword and ask people for referrals.

Sites You'll Find Helpful When Developing Your Products

Audio and Video Products
~ *http://mixiv.com/*

Teleseminar Services
~ *http://peggymccoll.audioacrobat.com*

Webinar Services
~ *www.maestroconference.com*
~ *www.maestromonth.com*

~ *www.gotomeeting.com*

~ *www.Webex.com*

~ *www.theWebinarpros.com*

Graphic Design

You can buy book jacket designs, Website templates, and packaging designs at: *www.killercovers.com.*

Audio and Video

You can download royalty-free video clips, animation, and photographs at these sites:

~ *www.istockphoto.com*

~ *www.bigstockphoto.com*

~ *www.fotosearch.com*

eBooks and Books

Several companies offer self-publishing and/or print-on-demand services and related services that can range from editing to e-mail and social media marketing campaigns:

~ *www.xlibris.com*

~ *www.iuniverse.com*

~ *www.lulu.com*

~ *www.outskirtspress.com*

~ *www.createspace.com*

You can upload your eBook to be accessed on the following sites.

~ *www.amazon.com*

~ *www.bn.com*

~ *www.ebooks.com*

~ *www.free-ebooks.net*

~ *www.gutenberg.org*

If you're unable to convert your Word document to a .pdf when you save the file for your eBook, you can use the application here:

~ *www.doc2pdf.net/converter* (Word to .pdf)

~ *www.softpedia.com/progDownload/CuteWriter-Download-12692.html*

To register your book's copyright:

~ If you live in the U.S.: *www.copyright.gov*

~ In Canada: *www.cb-cda.gc.ca/info/registration-e.html*

~ In Australia: *www.copyright.org.au*

~ In the UK: *www.copyrightservice.co.uk*

You can find professional ghostwriters and editors at:

~ *www.asja.org* (the American Society of Journalists and Authors)

~ *www.nancypeske.com* (Nancy is my ghostwriter)

You can find professional editors and copyeditors at:

~ *www.the-efa.org*

~ *www.elance.com*

~

You can find names of book editors and agents at these sites:

~ *www.agentquery.com*

~ *www.everyonewhosanyone.com*

~ *www.writers.net/agents.html*

~ *www.writers-free-reference.com/agents*

Services for Newsletters and eCourses

You'll need a list service to manage your e-mail list. Many of the shopping-cart services include this feature, but you can also use:

~ *www.aweber.com*

~ *www.icontact.com*

~ *www.netatlantic.com*

~ *www.constantcontact.com*

Shopping-Cart Services

~ *www.1shoppingcart.com*

~ *www.clickbank.com*

Sites That Will Help You Identify Potential Affiliates

You can check the popularity of particular Websites, which will help you identify potential affiliates, at:

~ *www.alexa.com*

~ *www.compete.com*

Sites That Will Help You With Website Hosting and Design

The following are services that allow you to reserve a domain name and buy hosting services. Some offer you free Website templates and design advice, too:

~ *www.smallbusiness.yahoo.com*

~ *www.godaddy.com*

~ *www.networksolutions.com*

~ *www.intuit.com*

I recommend these Website designers:

~ *www.3da.com:* Fernando Martinez

~ *www.onegraphic.com:* Colin Miller

This is a source for free Website templates:

~ *www.killersites.com*

This site features a product that offers help in building a subscriber list:

~ *www.trafficgeyser.com*

Sites That Will Help You With Landing-Page Design

Here are some sample landing pages to give you some ideas on how to lay out a landing page with all its many elements:

~ *www.moneyandspirituality.com*

~ *www.findsponsorsnow.com*

~ *www.psychologicaltriggers.com*

~ *www.teleseminarsecrets.com*

~ *www.viralexplosions.com*

Here are some copywriters who write landing pages:

~ *www.cariboodirectmarketing.com* (Al Henderson is my copywriter)

~ *www.thegaryhalbertletter.com*

~ *www.tednicholas.com*

~ *www.dankennedy.com*

~ *www.davidgarfinkel.com*

Sites Helpful for Promotion and Publicity

~ Bradley Communications 1 (Steve Harrison & Bill Harrison) Provide a variety of publications, services, and training events for authors, experts, entrepreneurs, nonprofit organizations, public relations professionals, and others to help them build their business and secure media publicity.

~ *www.rtir.com*

~ *www.nationalpublicitysummit.com*

~ *www.reporterconnection.com*

~ *www.freepublicity.com*

~ *www.milliondollarauthorclub.com*

These sites allow you to submit articles that are made available to Websites and e-mail newsletter owners looking for content. They usually have strict rules about how much promotional material can be included in the article, but you can always insert a link to your Website into your author biography if not the text of the article itself:

~ *www.ezinearticles.com*

~ *www.articlesbase.com*

~ *www.Buzzle.com*

~ *www.GoArticles.com*

~ *www.ArticleAlley.com*

~ *www.ArticleDashboard.com*

~ *www.selfgrowth.com*

~ *www.articlemarketer.com*

~ *www.isnare.com*

~ *www.ideamarketers.com*

~ *www.articlecity.com*

~ *www.articlehub.com*

~ *www.articlesfactory.com*

~ *www.marketing-seek.com*

~ *www.goarticles.com*

You can submit press releases to these sites:

~ *www.prWeb.com*

~ *www.24-7pressrelease.com*

~ *www.prfree.com*

~ *www.prleap.com*

~ *www.przoom.com*

~ *www.pr.com*

~ *www.1888pressrelease.com*

~ *www.prlog.org*

~ *www.prnewswire.com*

~ *www.i-newswire.com or www.newswire.ca* (in Canada)

You can upload your video to these sites, where it can be accessed free of charge by anyone:

~ *www.youtube.com*

~ *www.video.google.com*

~ *www.video.yahoo.com*

~ *www.atomfilms.com* (comedy only)

~ *www.twango.com*

You can learn about interview and media opportunities here:

~ *www.haro.com*: Help a Reporter Out or HARO is a service that sends out requests for anecdotes, talk show guests, and experts that come in from journalists, freelance writers, bloggers, and television and radio producers. Subscribe to services like this one to scout for opportunities to promote your brand and product.

~ *www.freepublicity.com*

~ *www.prleads.com*: Their PR service will send out press releases as well as send you leads from reporters.

~ *www.hasmarkservices.com*: Hasmark Services expertise is providing effective, industry leading online marketing solutions for authors, publishers, professionals, and experts who wish to create a prominent online presence to sell books, products, and services.

Important Social Media Sites

Although there are many social media sites now, these four are the most important to work with in order to get out the word about your viral explosion:

~ *www.facebook.com*

~ *www.linkedin.com*

~ *www.twitter.com*

~ *www.youtube.com*

Peggy McColl

My Websites are: *www.destinies.com* and *www.viralexplosions.com*

To view a promotional video I made for my book *Be a Dog with a Bone*, featuring my dog, Pablo, visit *www.youtube.com/peggymccoll*.

Index

About the Author

Peggy McColl is a *New York Times* best-selling author and an internationally recognized expert in the field of personal and professional development and Internet marketing.

As an entrepreneur, business owner, mentor, and professional speaker, Peggy has been inspiring individuals to pursue their personal and business objectives and achieve ultimate success.

She provides effective Internet marketing solutions for entrepreneurs, authors, publishers, professionals, and business owners who want to establish an online presence, achieve best-seller status, build their brand, and grow and/or expand their business online. You can find out more about Peggy at her Website, *www.destinies.com.*